T0088016

PAUL BROWN'S GHOST

How the Cleveland Browns and Cincinnati Bengals Are
Haunted by the Man Who Created Them

Jonathan Knight

SPORTS
PUBLISHING

Sports Publishing books may be purchased in bulk at special discounts for sales promotion, corporate gifts, fund-raising, or educational purposes. Special editions can also be created to specifications. For details, contact the Special Sales Department, Sports Publishing, 307 West 36th Street, 11th Floor, New York, NY 10018 or sportspubbooks@skyhorsepublishing.com.

Sports Publishing® is a registered trademark of Skyhorse Publishing, Inc.®, a Delaware corporation.

Visit our website at www.sportspubbooks.com.

10 9 8 7 6 5 4 3 2 1

Library of Congress Cataloging-in-Publication Data is available on file.

Cover design by Tom Lau
Cover photo credit Associated Press

ISBN: 978-1-68358-244-1
Ebook ISBN: 978-1-6835-8245-8

Printed in the United States of America

For Sherry—my favorite Burrito Buggy-loving Bobcat,
and the big sister I never had.

"Monsters are real, and ghosts are real, too. They live inside us, and sometimes, they win."
—Stephen King

Table of Contents

Preface and Acknowledgments

Dayton, Ohio, is a lot like Berlin.

That's almost certainly the first time *that* statement has ever been made, but stick with me.

As America has learned time and again, in the political landscape, Ohio is what's charmingly referred to as a "battleground state." And understandably so. It's a demographic goulash that seems to serve as a microcosm of American culture, containing most, if not all, of its primary socioeconomic components. Consequently, every few years, Ohio is napalmed with "And I Approved This Message" ads in the endless weeks that ultimately nose-dive into yet another bitter, exhausting election.

While politicos have been unapologetically trolling Ohio for the past several decades, the Gem City of Dayton has been a similar type of battleground for nearly as long. Not in terms of politics, but, rather, in the realm of professional football.

It's the point on the map at which two kingdoms of fanhood collide head-on—where Cleveland Browns Country meets Cincinnati Bengals Nation.

Geographically, it doesn't feel like the logical place for such an inter-section. Barely fifty miles from downtown Cincinnati, Dayton seems like it should be solidly in the Bengals' column. But Dayton has always maintained a bedrock foundation of old-school Browns fans who rooted for the team—and Paul Brown—long before the Bengals were even a tiger-striped glint in Brown's eye. They passed that loyalty on to their progeny, who then passed it on to theirs, even as the Bengals became more established and their fan base grew around them. Even now, mul-tiple generations later, the Browns have a strong enough presence in Dayton to keep the city's overall allegiance too close to call.

It certainly isn't the only place in Ohio where you'll see Hatfield/McCoy tendencies at gameday bars, but it's undoubtedly the capital of the Browns-Bengals rivalry and the junction point of a half century of hard feelings. Not unlike Berlin in the aftermath of World War II—where the political philosophies of East Germany and West Germany T-boned each other and set the geopolitical tone for the next four decades.

This is where I grew up—Dayton, that is, not Berlin. That would have been a very different book.

The son of native Clevelanders, I inherited my interest in Northeast Ohio sports and the Browns from my parents. And while Dayton was (and is) a relatively safe haven for a Cleveland sports fan, I still found myself regularly on the defensive for my football fandom choice.

Walking into school on autumn Monday mornings in the late 1980s, for instance, was often like trying to casually stroll across the 38th paral-lel. Depending on whom I saw and how Sunday's games went, I might be in for a verbal assault from my Who Dey brothers and sisters or take part in a jubilant barking frenzy with fellow Browns backers at any given moment.

And for me, this wasn't just a matter of catching the final scores Sun-day evening or the box scores on Monday morning. Living right on the edge (physically and psychologically) of the Cincinnati television mar-ket, I was exposed to more Bengals football than any young Browns fol-lower probably ever should have been. Back in the Mesozoic Era before DirecTV's Sunday Ticket, football television options were extremely limited. So when I wasn't watching the Browns, I pretty much had no other choice but to watch the archnemesis Bengals.

Consequently, a football version of Stockholm syndrome began to develop. Even when the Browns weren't playing, I'd feel an urge—a need, really—to watch the Bengals. And even now, I can't entirely explain why. While this exposure certainly didn't result in my actually *rooting* for the Bengals, it did inadvertently nurture a unique respect for them and their history. And, much later, a genuine understanding that both of these teams and their respective fan bases formed less a rivalry than a strange, tense family bond. Like a perpetually awkward holiday dinner that lasted four months every year. All stemming back to the man who, in essence, created both franchises.

In other words, my Dayton-as-Berlin childhood backdrop wound up putting me in a uniquely advantageous position to straddle these two worlds and tell a story that deeply affected both of them. And it's a doozy—for my money, the greatest ghost story in NFL history.

This is a Shirley Jackson-style haunting of not one franchise, but two, by arguably the most important figure in the history of pro football. In a league in which going from worst to first in one year is almost as common as a ligament sprain—and as the number of teams that have never won the Super Bowl keeps shrinking around them—for two separate teams connected by the same bloodline to be perpetually denied good fortune in such dramatic, yet different, ways under such consistently suspicious circumstances demands further investigation.

The book you're about to read sets out to do exactly that. We'll tiptoe into this haunted house together and try to solve the mystery of why these once-proud franchises can't seem to shake the specter that follows them like a shadow in a cemetery. In between the billowing curtains along the long, dark hallways, we'll examine portraits on the wall of the characters who defined—and, in some cases, defiled—the history of these teams. We'll enter dusty rooms and uncover old stories that explain the deep, fraternal connection between the Browns and Bengals and illustrate how this bond first shaped them and still continues to. We'll blow the cobwebs off some amazing encounters between these two teams . . . and a few genuinely dreadful ones. And while we'll discover spooky details and truly horrific episodes throughout, just like Scooby-Doo and Shaggy in their paranormal adventures, I think we'll have fun along the way.

I know I had a dabba-doo time putting this thing together. And like with any such journey, I couldn't have done it alone. I have to thank Julie Ganz from Skyhorse Publishing for believing in this crazy idea and then helping shepherd it into reality, along with all the gang at Sports Publishing, Inc. Also, shout-outs to all who offered encouragement and advice, especially good friends Seth Shaner, Roger Gordon, and Todd Stinchcomb, who each provided valuable insight and corrections along with much-needed enthusiasm. And special thanks to Kathryn "K-Nasty" Nesterov for her keen advice on design—and for teaching me that sometimes we speak in colors.

As always, the Ohio History Center's amazing archives and library in Columbus proved invaluable for the research that forms the backbone of the book. There are only a few places in this world at which I really feel at home, and—strange as it may sound—that's one of them.

And where would I be without the love, support, comradeship, and fart jokes provided by my two goofball sons, Zachary and Jacob, who keep things funny and messy and generally prevent me from sinking into my own head. Thanks, fellas . . . now put down your electronics and go read a book.

Speaking of encouragement, I also have to thank my wonderful and always-smarter sister Jeannine (who, coincidentally, has Cincinnati in the palm of her hand) and her rock-star family: Mike, Carter, and Evelyn—explaining clambakes to southwestern Ohio since 2006.

And of course, there are my parents, who continue to show everyone around them what true north is. My mom, for her ability to fix anything, including (and especially) people's lives. And my dad, for, among many other things, all the times when he'd climb up onto the roof to point the TV antenna toward Columbus to catch a fuzzy reception of the Browns game when all that was on was the Bengals. Then coming back down and watching it with me.

From those childhood days in Dayton right up to today, it's been a pretty good life—ghosts and all.

Prologue:
August 5, 1991

For football fans, August is like Christmastime.

As the back-to-school sales pop up like afternoon thunderstorms, football teams begin to gather on the heat-singed grass of practice fields in mesh jerseys and shorts to begin preparing for a new season.

It's one of the first signs that summer's vice-like grip is waning and that the bright color and cool days of autumn are just over the horizon. And through these hot, muggy afternoons, fans begin counting the days until the games—at each point of the triad of organized levels—finally begin. Optimism and excitement run rampant, and even for teams and fans with no real competitive hopes, just the return of football seems to satisfyingly scratch a six-month itch.

It is, therefore, only appropriate that the father of modern football shuffled off this mortal coil at precisely this time of year. He left a world revving up for a new season, whetting its insatiable appetite for the game he'd helped weave into the fabric of the culture and mold into a generational touchstone.

At 4:20 a.m. on Monday, August 5, 1991, at his home in the Cincinnati suburb of Indian Hill, Paul Brown died of complications from pneumonia. Considering the menagerie of health problems the eighty-two-year-old had endured over the previous year, it didn't come as a huge surprise. He'd been hospitalized the previous December with a blood clot in his leg, then came down with pneumonia in May and, over the next three months, would fight a losing battle.

Along with the medical prognoses, there were other signs that all was not right with this man who'd remained dedicated to the game for better than sixty years. He'd missed the NFL owners meetings in March and hadn't been able to attend training camp practices that summer. Even more telling, the previous October, he hadn't made the trip for a much-anticipated Monday-night game between the Cincinnati Bengals and Cleveland Browns—the two teams he'd essentially created.

August 5 would be the twenty-third day of training camp for the Browns—whom Paul Brown had constructed in 1946—and the nineteenth day of camp for the Bengals—whom he'd created in 1968. In the decades that followed, both teams had enjoyed much success and had established themselves as two respected franchises in the National Football League. And both considered Paul Brown their George Washington.

The NFL itself owed a considerable debt to Paul Brown. True, it had been founded thirty years before Brown became a part of it, but the vast majority of its success branched from his arrival and the way his techniques and philosophies changed the game. Even today, as pro football nears its centennial, its history can be clearly designated into two parts: before Paul Brown and after.

Before, it was the Wild West, only not quite as civilized. Teams were largely unorganized and undisciplined, and games were aboriginal cacophonies of random violence. After, they were symphonies, carefully structured and plotted out, each play mirroring a military action, with a week's worth of preparation and thought contained within. In the blink of an eye, football became an exercise in precision that made it far more entertaining and appealing to mass audiences—and, not for nothing, one that would eventually fit perfectly within the frame of a television screen. "Paul Brown didn't invent the game of football," *Sport Magazine* declared five years before he died. "He was just the first to take it seriously."

Even his death was businesslike and efficient. Thinking ahead, he'd instructed Sam Wyche, head coach of the Bengals, not to disrupt the team's training camp were Brown to take a turn for the worse. And sure enough, after a few emotional words to the team the morning Brown passed, Bengals practice went on as scheduled. There would be no com-memorative patches on the uniforms, no arm bands on their sleeves. Even the nominal transition of power was silent and smooth: as he'd been groomed to do for years, son Mike would take over the mantle of team owner. The only indication that anything was different were the letters "PB" on Boomer Esiason's helmet, which the quarterback had penned in black magic marker in between the signature stripes that Brown himself had selected as a design concept ten years before.

Ironically, there was more pomp and circumstance in Cleveland than Cincinnati. That evening, Cleveland Municipal Stadium—where Brown had begun his NFL career one month short of forty-five years before—observed a moment of silence before a Browns exhibition game.

As the news broke that Monday morning, the city of Massillon, where the Paul Brown Story truly began, snapped to action. City officials contacted the American Legion to ask about the proper procedure for requesting permission to lower the city's flags in respect. When told only the governor or the president of the United States could authorize such an action, a call was made to Columbus. Permission was quickly granted, and, by afternoon, every flag in the city was at half-staff.

His funeral in Massillon two days later drew the type of gathering you'd generally only see at the annual Pro Football Hall of Fame induc-tion up State Route 30 in Canton. Legendary coaches and players all came to pay their respects, and the tiny church overflowed with people, with hundreds more gathered outside and across the street.

The NFL's current and past commissioners sat side by side. His pall-bearers—each a former player, almost perfectly personifying the differ-ent chapters of Brown's coaching career—gathered near the front. And in the fifth row sat the enigmatic, silver-haired showman who'd nearly ended Paul Brown's career and ultimately became the Moriarty to his Sherlock—or, perhaps a better analogy, the Bernardo to Brown's Riff. Understandably, following years of vitriol between the pair, after he'd heard the news, Art Modell didn't call the Brown family to offer his con-dolences, feeling it would be inappropriate. Nor was he sure if he'd attend the funeral. But attend he did and then—true to form—denied ever hesitating in the first place.

The brevity of the service itself was a fitting tribute to Brown. No choir. No eulogy. No heartfelt speeches. In and out in eighteen minutes flat. Not for the last time, it was as if Paul Brown were speaking from beyond the grave: *Back to business, everybody. No big deal.* "All of us are important," Brown used to like to say, "but none of us are necessary."

Sage words of wisdom that are generally true. But for pro football to succeed and become the corporate behemoth it is today, Paul Brown was indeed necessary. Without him, NFL history would have unfolded dramatically different, perhaps with it not becoming its own billion-dollar industry that claimed ownership of every Sunday six months of the year.

And certainly, neither the Cleveland Browns nor Cincinnati Bengals would ever have existed without Paul Brown. Just like any death of a father, his passing brought on a time of reflection for the sons—bookended by a sense of anxiety as to what would come next.

The Bengals, for whom Paul Brown remained the face and driving force behind until the day he died, said there was nothing to fear. The public, the remaining oracles of the front office insisted, would notice little if any change in the Bengals organization, on the field and off.

But, of course, there would be.

Even the Browns, to whom Paul Brown had not been connected for nearly three decades, would feel the ground move beneath their feet. Perhaps not immediately, but dramatically and permanently.

For both of these franchises, at the dawn of the bright promise of a new season, there were dark thunderheads on the horizon.

A storm was on its way.

1

Beginnings and Endings

1944-1969

On that bright summer morning in 1991 when Paul Brown was laid to rest, neither the Cleveland Browns nor the Cincinnati Bengals was known as an NFL powerhouse. But they were highly respected teams that had enjoyed more than their fair share of success.

Combined, they'd made thirty-three postseason appearances, including thirteen trips to the NFL's title game. Things had really gotten cooking over the previous decade, with the Browns and Bengals piling up eleven trips to the playoffs in eleven years, with seven division titles, five appearances in the American Football Conference Championship, and a pair of Super Bowl trips. They'd never been more consistent or more respected.

In a heartbeat, that all changed.

August 5, 1991, became a demarcation line in both teams' histories, one that's difficult to believe or comprehend. By all appearances, when Paul Brown died, he took a good part of the two NFL teams he helped create with him.

Consider each franchise's all-time records, before and after:

Before Paul Brown's death:

Bengals   171–168–1 (.504)
Browns   385–226–13 (.627)

After Paul Brown's death:

Bengals   180–249–3 (.420)
Browns   124–260 (.323)

That's a drop of nearly ten percentage points for the Bengals and a whopping thirty for the Browns. Put another way, before Paul Brown left us, the typical Bengals season ended with an 8–8 record. Afterward, it was 6–10. For the Browns, the dichotomy was even more dramatic: 10–6 to 5–11.

Compared to the teams' relatively heady accomplishments prior to August 5, 1991, in the forty-plus combined seasons between the teams since, the Browns and Bengals have reached the postseason nine times in total—meaning, on average, one of the two teams would make the playoffs just once every five to six years. And of those nine appearances, only once has one of Paul Brown's former teams managed a victory: the Browns on New Year's Day 1995. Since then, the Browns have played in a grand total of one postseason game (losing it, naturally), while the Bengals have lost all seven playoff games they've played, including four on their home field. Worse still for both teams, four of those nine combined postseason losses have come to the mutually despised Pittsburgh Steelers.

A logical person would attempt to pass this off as mere coincidence. Surely it must simply be a combination of unrelated factors that have led to such a drastic hairpin turn for both franchises. And it's just coincidence that it happened to coincide with the passing of Paul Brown.

But how can you explain the same comedy of errors played out over nearly three decades by a multitude of casts of characters? Playing in different stadiums, with different players and different coaches, under the direction of different front offices, and even under the thumb of different owners, they've continually fallen prey to the same fate. Sometimes crushing, often comic.

When does a parade of coincidences cease to be coincidence? When do you stop trying to rationally explain the inexplicable? When do you begin to think that what's troubling these teams can't be fixed by standard procedures?

At what point do you consider the possibility that Paul Brown is haunting the two teams he created?

The year before Paul Brown died, the Bengals won the AFC Central Division for the second time in three years and cruised to a blowout win in a first-round playoff game.

The year he died, they dropped to 3–13, the worst mark in team history, and would not post a winning record for an incredible fourteen straight seasons—topped only by the New Orleans Saints' first twenty seasons as the worst stretch in league history.

The parallel to the Browns' downfall is even creepier. The day that Paul Brown died, a new head coach marched onto the sideline in Cleveland for the very first time. This marked the beginning of the five most unpleasant—some might even say "horrific"—years for any team in Cleveland sports history. And when they were over, the team ceased to exist.

Were it just one team that entered a rough patch, perhaps it could be explained away and passed off as coincidental timing. But both? And starting literally the very day that their mutual patriarch died?

The Cleveland Browns and Cincinnati Bengals didn't die on August 5, 1991. Today, they're very much alive—if not always well—and each autumn Sunday, they take the field before large crowds in crystalline football palaces.

But in the years that have followed the death of their creator—for one, its namesake, for the other, its founder—they've seemingly never recovered. It seems their souls died along with him, and they've spent decades trying to get them back.

***

In a way, it's almost biblical.

The Cleveland Browns and the Cincinnati Bengals are Isaac and Ishmael, sired by the same father but then set off to form completely separate, competing cultures. Only instead of Jews and Muslims, we have the Dawg Pound and the Jungle.

Indeed, Paul Brown is the Abraham of football in the gridiron-bonkers state of Ohio. And not just at the professional level. He essentially put the state on the map at each stage of the game over an epic sixty-year career.

His first job was at tiny Severn Prep in Maryland, where he won sixteen of eighteen games in two seasons. But his career truly began in 1932, when he was named the head football coach at Massillon High School, his alma mater. He took over a program that had managed just a single victory the year before he arrived and promptly turned it into a national powerhouse. After completing a 5–4–1 record in Brown's first season, the Tigers jumped to 8–2 in his second, 9–1 in his third, and then lost just one game over the next six years as Massillon won five state titles and became the high school football capital of America. A mammoth new football stadium was constructed in 1937 and still stands today as a monument to what Brown built in Massillon. By 1940, the Tigers were drawing an average of 18,000 fans to their games in a town that consisted of 26,000 people.

When Ohio State University's head coaching position opened up that year, a groundswell of coaches and fans recommended Brown as the Buckeyes' next leader. He was hired and, at the age of thirty-three, became the youngest coach in the history of what's now known as the Big Ten. Just like at Massillon, he immediately improved the Buckeyes' fortunes, winning six of eight games in 1941, followed by a 9–1 record and OSU's first national championship in 1942.

After a letdown season in 1943, with the US embroiled in World War II, Brown was commissioned as a naval officer at the Great Lakes Naval Training Station. There, he served as the coach of a football team made up of recruits that would play colleges and other service teams. It was a temporary gig for Brown, who'd intended to return to Ohio State once the war was over and build a college football dynasty in Columbus.

Instead, in a surprising plot twist, he wound up creating modern professional football.

Arch Ward, a Chicago newspaper columnist, approached Brown with an offer. Ward, best known for creating baseball's All-Star Game a decade before, was launching a professional football league to rival the established NFL. Knowing Brown's reputation as a coach, particularly in Ohio, Ward wanted him to lead the team that would play in Cleveland.

Brown was wary at first, subscribing to the general perception of the time that the professional game wasn't real football and that the college game was more appealing. But when Ohio State was lukewarm about him returning and the offer became too good to refuse, he decided to make what he himself called a "rash move." He signed a lucrative five-year contract with this newfangled football enterprise—which included a percentage of ownership of the team—nineteen months before it would play its first game.

Still stationed at Great Lakes for another year, Brown remotely oversaw construction of the early components of the fledging franchise. Step one was to name the team. The *Cleveland Plain Dealer* held a write-in contest in which fans would enter suggestions. Whoever submitted the winning entry would win a $1,000 war bond. The paper received more than 8,000 entries, and "Panthers" was selected in June of 1945.

Two months later, a gentleman came to team owner Arthur McBride and explained that he'd owned a semipro team called the Cleveland Panthers in the 1930s and that the name belonged to him. The legend is that when Brown discovered there'd been an unsuccessful football team by that name, he ordered that a new name be cooked up because he didn't want there to be any association with a loser. In reality, the owner of the original Panthers demanded that the new team pay him several thousand dollars for permission to use the name. Brown and McBride said no, and another write-in contest was held. This time, several fans suggested an homage to their new coach who, though just thirty-seven years old, was already a legend.

So on August 14, 1945—the same day Japan surrendered to end World War II—the team was officially named the Cleveland Browns. Still a year away from taking the field, with Brown as the headliner, they were already the biggest show in town. So much so that the NFL's Cleveland Rams, who'd struggled to build a fan base in their nine years of existence, skedaddled to Los Angeles the following January—just weeks after winning the league championship.

Over the next year, Brown built his team. There was no draft, no player personnel director, no scouting department. He contacted several players he'd either coached or coached against over the years and offered them contracts. He won over Northwestern star quarterback Otto Graham, convincing him to sign a contract with the Browns rather than the Detroit Lions, who'd selected him in the NFL draft. He signed Lou Groza and Lin Houston before they returned from the war. He welcomed a handful of Rams players who didn't want to move to Los Angeles and won a court case that freed them from their contracts. Most significantly, more interested in winning than he was in conforming to certain practices of much of pro sports of the day, Brown had no issue with signing black players, and he brought in stars like Bill Willis, Marion Motley, and Horace Gillom.

Employing a robust staff of six assistants—three times what most teams had and the first staff to work year-round—Brown instilled aspects of the game that today are as accepted as yard lines and goalposts. Showing and discussing films of the previous game with players. Personality and intelligence tests. Studying opponents' game films. Fines for being late to practice and lost playbooks. Classroom-like preparation for each game. Football was a business, and Paul Brown was a cold and calculating CEO.

Brown and his Browns were ahead of the curve in pro football and light years ahead of the wobbly AAFC. Over the next four seasons, the Browns only lost four of their fifty-four games, rolling to four consecutive league titles and a level of dominance that actually accelerated the AAFC's demise. When the league folded after the 1949 season, the Browns were one of three AAFC teams that were enveloped into the NFL. Most expected Brown to get his comeuppance at the grown-ups table, but essentially nothing changed. His team cruised to a 10–2 record, avenged its only two defeats with a playoff victory over the New York Giants, then won a dramatic—and symbolic—championship game over the Rams, who'd fled Cleveland in the wake of the Browns' arrival five years before.

Several of the faces changed, but the Browns remained a power-house, reaching the NFL Championship Game in each of their first six seasons in the NFL, winning back-to-back crowns in 1954 and 1955. But when Otto Graham retired after the '55 season, the Browns dipped a bit and never truly returned to the same level of dominance. The drafting of Syracuse running back Jim Brown the following year kept the Browns near the top of the standings, but after a blowout loss to Detroit in the 1957 title game and an ugly playoff defeat to New York in 1958, they would never again reach the postseason under Paul Brown.

Over the next four years, Brown, once heralded as a genius, began to be labeled as an out-of-touch relic. He seemed to have lost his knack for identifying talent, reflected by his trading away a handful of linemen who would anchor the defensive line that would lead the Green Bay Packers to a dynasty of their own in the 1960s. He passed on signing Johnny Unitas and released future Hall of Fame quarterback Len Dawson after minimal use in two seasons.

His harsh treatment of and comments to players—which may have been considered effective while winning championships—now gener-ated resentment and fear. A player would return to the sideline after making a mistake and see Brown's stony gaze, as he snarled things like, "Don't tell me that's how the great ones do it," and, "Where are you going to work next year?"

Those methods had obviously worked over the years. But times, players, and the game itself were changing. As writer George Cantor put it in his book *Paul Brown: The Man Who Invented Modern Football,* Brown had become "a big band kind of guy in a rock 'n' roll world."

The Browns finished just above .500 and never genuinely chal-lenged for a conference crown from 1959 through 1962. It wasn't that the Browns were bad, they just weren't living up to the lofty standards they'd set for themselves. Which likely would have been tolerable under any of the previous regimes of ownership Brown had worked with. But in 1961, a slick New York advertising man bought the team.

And here is where things got interesting.

***

"I'm buying it," Art Modell told Paul Brown, "because of you."

When Modell purchased the Browns for $4 million in January 1961, nobody knew who he was. And neither Brown nor anyone else could have possibly known what impact he would have on the coach, the team, and the NFL itself.

Though Brown didn't know Modell, he had no reason to expect things to be different than they'd been. Brown was used to having complete control over every aspect of the team, granted totalitarian authority by absentee owners who were content to sit back and let the money roll in rather than meddle with the master.

And by all appearances, Modell was awed by Brown. He was a self-proclaimed football buff who knew and appreciated everything Brown had accomplished. He made Brown a wealthy man by buying out his shares of the team (for roughly $500,000), extended Brown's contract, and nearly doubled his salary.

But when the rubber hit the road, the seams began to show. As the Browns staggered to 8–5–1 and 7–6–1 records in Modell's first two years as owner, he would complain in the press box about Brown's play-calling. The owner pampered his players with drinks and dinners, which irritated Brown, but not as much as Modell's incessant questions to players about whether they thought the coach was treating them right.

Not unlike the Cuban Missile Crisis, things came to a head in the fall of 1962. Modell guaranteed the Browns would win the championship, putting further pressure on the coach by way of the media and fans. Brown flustered Modell by not consulting him when he traded running back Bobby Mitchell to Washington to acquire rookie running back Ernie Davis. After Davis was diagnosed with leukemia before his first season could begin and only had months to live, Brown said Modell pressured him into playing the kid in a game to give him a thrill before he died. Modell denied it, but the hard feelings between the two men had developed into an unbridgeable chasm. Ratcheting up the tension, the Browns slogged to a third-place finish, well off the pace.

On the first Monday of 1963, Modell called Brown into his office. Modell outlined how the team had struggled in recent years and stated that seven players had come to him and said they wouldn't return the following season if Brown was still the head coach.

He was making a change, Modell explained, and Paul Brown would no longer be the head coach of the team named after him. Brown was understandably stunned.

To this day, versions of exactly how the story played out differ. Brown remembers Modell telling him, "This team can never fully be mine as long as you are here because whenever anyone thinks of the Cleveland Browns, they think of you. Every time I come to the Stadium, I feel that I am invading your domain, and from now on there can only be one dominant image." Later, Brown said he'd heard that Modell had told a friend that "Firing Paul Brown will be my claim to fame."

Brown left Modell's office in a daze. Adding insult to injury, he claims that Modell callously had the contents of Brown's office packed into a cardboard box and shipped to his home. Modell's version is that when Brown came back to collect his belongings from his office, he saw his assistants watching game film and preparing for the new season as if nothing had happened. This had apparently upset Brown so much that he'd left without his things, and Modell figured he'd have them delivered if Brown wasn't going to take them himself.

It was a stunning moment, one that shook the foundation of the Cleveland Browns. The news broke during a prolonged newspaper strike in Cleveland, preventing many of the details from getting out (which, some conspiracy theorists suggest, is exactly what Modell wanted and had timed it accordingly). In an era in which television was still in its infancy and radio was the only other real source of news, fans didn't quite know how to handle what had happened. There were even legitimate questions of whether the team would or could still be called the "Browns." Modell brushed it aside. "This is the image we've created," he said. "We're still the Browns."

Still, there were rumors that Modell never liked the name and hated the idea of his team still carrying Paul Brown's legacy. Some say this is where the unfounded origin story about the Browns being named for champion boxer Joe Louis—a.k.a. "The Brown Bomber"—came from. The story goes that after he fired Paul Brown, Modell began floating the Joe Louis angle to try to shift the team's identity away from Brown.

There's no proof to support the theory, but considering Modell's modus operandi—and what was to come—it has a ring of truth to it.

Nevertheless, the Cleveland Browns would continue their journey as the Cleveland Browns. But without their George Washington.

***

Like an overthrown dictator (an apt metaphor, some felt), Paul Brown fled his football capital and lived in exile.

He and his wife moved to La Jolla, California—essentially the farthest spot in the continental US from Cleveland. Still being paid by the team, holding the hollow role of "vice president," he played golf and traveled the world. For most, it would be an idyllic retirement. For Paul Brown, it was the low point of his life.

He yearned to get back into the game, but under the right circumstances. He turned down opportunities to coach, first in Philadelphia, then in Los Angeles, because he didn't like the ownership situation of either team. He certainly wasn't going to get involved with any more Art Modells. He wanted a situation similar to his early years in Cleveland, when he had total control over the team, on the field and off. And with the foundation of the rival American Football League opening new markets and spurring a wave of new teams in new cities in the NFL, Brown began to consider investing his own money into starting up an expansion team. That way *he* could be the Art Modell.

His son Mike put together a comprehensive study of a handful of cities that didn't already have pro football, and he and his father quickly agreed on the best opportunity: Cincinnati. Not just because the Queen City was the most appealing for economic and geographic reasons, but also because it would enable Brown to leverage his reputation and connections in Ohio to get the ball rolling.

In the fall of 1965, Brown mentioned the idea to a well-connected friend. His friend got word to James Rhodes, the governor of Ohio, who was just as excited and flew to California to meet with Brown and discuss the possibility. Rhodes set up meetings, and Brown shuttled back and forth between La Jolla and Cincinnati to meet with prospective ownership partners.

While most were enthusiastic, there was still much maneuvering to be done. One of the biggest obstacles for most of the other cities clawing for an expansion team was a suitable stadium. Brown's group spearheaded construction of a new, multipurpose downtown ballpark along the Ohio River. The tricky part was getting Major League Baseball's Cincinnati Reds to agree to move in and play their games there, as well. When Reds owner Bill DeWitt dug in his heels about staying at historic Crosley Field, Brown and Company put together a separate group of investors (several of whom were already investing in Cincinnati's football enterprise) to purchase the Reds from DeWitt. With the purchase completed, the Reds on board, and the new stadium—appropriately to be named "Riverfront"—on target for a 1970 opening, all the stars had aligned.

The NFL and AFL had each added an expansion team in 1965, and the following year, after the leagues agreed to merge, both committed to adding one more new team before the merger occurred in 1970. The NFL selected New Orleans as its new team in 1966, and, on May 24, 1967, the AFL announced that Cincinnati would be the home of its final addition. Better still, after two seasons, the Bengals would merge into the NFL along with the rest of the league. Officially, the ownership for the new team hadn't been announced, but Paul Brown's group was the more obvious choice over one led by former University of Cincinnati basketball coach John Wiethe.

NFL Commissioner Pete Rozelle called Cincinnati's effort to land a team the "most intense in pro football history." And, in a fitting touch of irony, one of the key players in helping Cincinnati—and ultimately Paul Brown—get the franchise was Art Modell, who had advised the Cincinnati contingent on several moves throughout the process. In jovial photo ops following the announcement, Governor Rhodes praised Modell's leadership and thanked him for "coaching Cincinnati to victory."

Of course, Rhodes wasted no time bringing up the possibility of a Battle of Ohio between Modell's Browns and Cincinnati's as-yet-unnamed entity. "This can be the greatest rivalry in all of football," Rhodes declared, "and that's what we want it to be."

Having to share some of the credit with Modell must have gnawed at Brown, but he was in no position to complain. Everything had come together beautifully, and 1967 became one of the most fulfilling years of his life. Later that summer, he was inducted into the new Pro Football Hall of Fame in Canton, just twelve miles from where his coaching career began. The induction ceremony was his first public appearance since leaving the Browns more than four years earlier, representing his triumphant reemergence into football. And, in what would prove to be another spooky twist, Brown was inducted on August 5—exactly twenty-four years to the day before he died.

In September, Brown's circle of investors was handed the keys to the new franchise. The price tag was $7.5 million, although—in a detail that's hilarious by today's standards—the team wouldn't share any of the league's television revenue until its third season. As general manager and head coach, Brown would have as much control as he did in Cleveland. And while John Sawyer was elected team president, there was no majority stockholder for Brown to answer to. It was an ideal situation, and Brown knew it. After a sabbatical of almost five years, he was back in the game. "This is like coming home," he said at the introductory press conference. "I'm living again."

The first order of business was to settle on a name for the team. Just as with the Browns two decades before, a naming contest was held, a winning entry was selected, and then instantly thrown out. In this case, the most popular choice was "Buckeyes," which was obviously never going to fly. Not only would Ohio State have certainly taken issue, but Brown & Co. wisely wanted the new club's appeal to extend beyond Ohio's borders into Kentucky and Indiana.

Brown suggested "Tigers" as an homage to Princeton University, where two of his partners had attended, or, more likely, as a nostalgic nod to his glory days at Massillon. Everyone liked the idea but thought the name was too common. They refined it to "Bengals," pointing out a connection to a not-terribly-successful semipro Cincinnati team in the late 1930s (which undermines the tale behind the Browns' selection-of-a-name episode and Paul Brown's insistence on his new club not being associated with an unsuccessful old team). Not coincidentally, the team adopted the same black-and-orange color scheme as Massillon. The helmets themselves were as minimalist as the Browns' logo-less lids—a blank orange slate with "Bengals" printed in narrow black letters arching across the sides. It was bread-and-butter, but that was by design. "Nothing is worse," Brown declared, "than a bad team with a crazy-looking uniform." That would come later.

Aside from the similar approach to fashion, it was a very different landscape in which Paul Brown would construct his second pro football franchise. Those who thought the game had evolved beyond Brown's expertise in his final years in Cleveland predicted disaster in Cincinnati. "Paul will find the game is much more complicated than when he left it," one coach told a reporter anonymously and condescendingly. "He could be eligible for Social Security before he fields a team that wins half its games."

Indeed, this wouldn't be like the construction of the original Browns in the freewheeling chaos of the waning days of World War II. Things were much more structured now, and Brown wouldn't have the inside track of earmarking talent from his days at Massillon and Ohio State. The initial edition of the Bengals consisted primarily of rookies fresh out of college and castoffs from other clubs. Most casual observers figured Paul Brown had bitten off more than he could chew. To them, it looked like a coach who had watched the game pass him by was now being saddled with an overmatched team that couldn't compete at the professional level, even in what many considered to be the "inferior" AFL.

Also, now as an owner, Brown kept a closer eye on the purse strings. One of his first hires was Al LoCasale as personnel director, who'd spend just a year with the Bengals before departing for a three-decade career building legendary teams for Al Davis's Oakland/Los Angeles/Oakland Raiders. LoCasale wanted the Bengals to hire three full-time college scouts, but Brown decided they couldn't afford that (remember, the Bengals were essentially living off of unemployment checks until the Brinks truck with TV money came rolling in). So his assistant coaches doubled as scouts. It was a marginal decision at the time, but its precedent would echo louder in the years to come.

Despite all the strikes against them, Brown and his young Bengals surprised many of their critics. They won two of their first three games—including their first at the University of Cincinnati's crackerbox Nippert

Stadium, which would serve as their home field until Riverfront was ready. The dark reality of expansion quickly settled in with a seven-game losing streak, and the Bengals finished 3–11.

Stockpiling smart draft picks and more young talent, Brown's squad won its first three games in 1969 and surged into first place in the West Division. The third was a thrilling victory over the eventual Super Bowl-champion Kansas City Chiefs, which inspired President Richard Nixon—a big football fan and longtime follower of the AFL—to write Brown a letter of congratulations. Injuries took their toll, and the Bengals only managed one more victory in their next eleven games, though it was a blowout win over a strong Raiders team that represented its only loss that season. The Bengals' growth was apparent, and Brown was named AFL Coach of the Year. A burgeoning fan base anticipated what might happen after the merger the next year. The optimism percolated when 49,000 season tickets were sold for the Bengals' first NFL season at Riverfront.

Meanwhile, along the state's northern border, followers of Paul Brown's first NFL team were equally optimistic at the dawn of the 1970s. The Browns had reached the NFL Championship Game four times in the past six seasons, and there was no reason to expect this level of success to taper off in the new era.

Paul Brown's old team and new team were on a collision course. One of the most unique—if not intense—rivalries in football history was about to begin.

2

The Haunting Begins

1991-1998

Just as they'd stood on the crest of a new era upon the AFL/NFL merger, the Browns and Bengals both saw the 1991 season as a delineating mark in their respective histories.

While essentially nothing had changed on the field, for the first time, the Bengals would begin a season without their owner and founder. The Browns, meanwhile, had just gone all-in with a new head coach that Art Modell assured everyone would be the last one he'd ever hire.

God knew the Browns needed some new leadership. A marvelous run in the second half of the 1980s that saw the team reach the postseason in five consecutive seasons had come to a record-scratch end in 1990. An aging team stitched together by declining talent and failed draft picks limped to a 2–3 record out of the gate before an eight-game losing streak underlined just how far it had fallen. Bud Carson—who'd been the head coach for a mere twenty-five games—was fired midseason, and offensive coordinator Jim Shofner grabbed the wheel of an eighteen-wheel semi barreling downhill with no brakes. When the bloodletting was finally over, the Browns finished with a 3–13 record—the worst in their history—and clearly needed to rebuild the franchise brick by brick.

The man selected to do the masonry was a thirty-eight-year-old wunderkind coordinator, who'd actually already interviewed for the Browns' head coaching job when Carson got the gig two years earlier. He was the hottest assistant in the league, having constructed a dominating defense that helped the New York Giants win a pair of Super Bowls. His name was—swelling drumroll and dramatic trumpet blast—Bill Belichick.

To the modern ear, this sounds like the beginning of a fairy tale. Belichick's name is the twenty-first-century equivalent of "Lombardi" (or, depending on the audience, perhaps "Voldemort"). Since the Browns were the first to recognize his potential and give him his first head coaching job, it's logical to anticipate the team instantly returning to a new era of excellence and dominance. (Essentially what happened in Pittsburgh when Bill Cowher—the runner-up in the Browns' coaching search—was hired a year later. It was the first of countless "what-ifs" melancholic Browns fans would wrestle with in the decades to come.)

However, the Belichick of the 1990s was not the Belichick he would become. In the parlance of *Saturday Night Live*, he wasn't ready for prime time and needed several more years to work through his flaws and figure things out. Unfortunately for the Browns and their fans, those training-pants years were in Cleveland, where all of the sour aspects of the Belichick experience took center stage, with very few of the bottom-line benefits to balance them out.

In many ways, Belichick was a modern version of Paul Brown—a stern, icy disciplinarian whose whole world was football and who wasn't at all interested in appeasing players (or even entertaining fans, for that matter). His low, robotic voice and monosyllabic answers to thoughtful questions made it clear this wasn't someone you'd want to have a beer with or invite to a cocktail party. Or be friends with at all, really.

Not like, say, the effervescent Sam Wyche, who entered his eighth season as the Bengals' head coach in 1991 feeling secure and confident, even though his tenure had modeled a Kings Island roller coaster. The ups and downs were almost manic, as his teams would swing back and forth between title contender and nonentity, sometimes in a single afternoon. Twice he'd rallied his team from a last-place finish one year to a division title the next. Such was the case in 1990, as the Bengals navigated another wildly inconsistent season to win their last two games in dramatic fashion and capture the AFC Central Division crown. With most of the key components coming back, the Bengals were still considered the favorite in the division in 1991 and still a legitimate Super Bowl contender. Which makes what happened next so remarkable.

It started on opening day in Denver, where the Cincinnati defense was shredded by longtime Browns nemesis John Elway in a 45–14 defeat. As lopsided as the loss was, it wasn't until Week Two that the alarm bells started to ring. Playing the same Houston Oilers team that the Bengals had throttled in a playoff game eight months earlier, Cincinnati was once again pounded, this time on its own home field before a national audience on a Sunday night, 30–7. For the first time in six years, the Bengals had lost their first two games.

Up next was the first-ever Browns-Bengals game that didn't involve Paul Brown. And appropriately, it was a memorable one. On an unseasonably hot and muggy September afternoon in Cleveland, the Browns parlayed an early safety into an 11–3 fourth-quarter lead. The Bengals struck back with ten quick points to surge ahead by two with less than seven minutes left. The Browns regained possession at their own twelve with three minutes remaining and, after sputtering most of the afternoon, began a frenzied drive downfield. They plowed into field-goal range, and with four seconds left, Matt Stover's kick from forty-five yards sailed just barely past the outstretched arms of Cincinnati cornerback Eric Thomas and, at the last moment, hooked through the uprights. It gave the Browns an emotional 14–13 victory, their first over the Bengals in nearly three years. On this balmy September Sunday, Paul Brown smiled on his original team.

With that, the Bengals hit terminal velocity. Five more losses would follow for Sam Wyche's group, and the defending division champs stood at a franchise-worst 0–8 when the Browns came to a chilly Riverfront Stadium for the rematch the first weekend of November. While the Bengals spiraled, Cleveland proved refreshingly competent and relatively resurgent under Belichick, standing at 4–4, having already surpassed its 1990 win total. It was a case of two teams heading in opposite directions colliding head-on. And the ensuing result may have been a golden example of a supernatural entity intervening to swing the outcome of a sporting event.

Propelled by a pair of short touchdown runs by bruising fullback Kevin Mack, the Browns roared to a 14–3 lead midway through the second quarter and were poised to cruise to an easy victory. But the beleaguered Bengals persevered, and a pair of Boomer Esiason scoring tosses propelled the home team into the lead early in what became a back-and-forth second half. After a third Mack score put the Browns ahead by a point, the Bengals answered with a field goal to go ahead, 23–21, early in the fourth quarter.

Then things got weird.

In the final five minutes, the Browns had four separate chances to take the lead, and all four went awry, under notably mysterious conditions. A determined march to the Cincinnati 15 fell apart when the sure-handed Mack fumbled. On the next possession, a forty-seven-yard field-goal attempt by Matt Stover—who'd defeated the Bengals seven weeks earlier and had made ten straight—swayed left at the last possible moment and hit the upright, denying the Browns another opportunity to go ahead with 1:56 remaining.

Not to be denied, the Browns got the ball back with just over a minute left and quickly marched back into Cincinnati territory. It appeared the Bengals' ninth straight loss was in the bag when, from the Cincinnati 24, quarterback Bernie Kosar spotted wide receiver Brian Brennan— who possessed a pair of the most dependable hands in franchise history—wide open in the end zone. Kosar's pass was right on the money, but somehow the ball bounced off Brennan's right shoulder pad and fell to the ground, incomplete. Stunning as Brennan's uncharacteristic drop was, it seemed it wouldn't matter. Seconds later, Stover jogged back onto the field, both to redeem himself for his earlier unlucky break and to repeat his heroics from two months before.

But his chip-shot attempt from thirty-four yards out never got airborne. Eric Thomas—who'd come within a Bengal tiger whisker of blocking Stover's game winner in September—broke through the right side and smothered the kick as the clock hit zero. The Browns staggered off the field, having suffered a defeat that would haunt them for the rest of the season.

"I can't say I've ever been involved in a game where you have that much go against you at the end of the game," Kosar said afterward. And sure enough, the Browns lost whatever modest mojo they'd had coming into the game, losing six of their last eight—several in similarly soul-crushing fashion—to finish 6–10.

Across the Riverfront carpet, the Bengals jubilantly celebrated their first triumph in nearly a year. One that, in retrospect, may have come with a little help from their founder intervening to balance the scales. "I have a feeling PB had something to do with this," Boomer Esiason said. "I think he was watching over us a little."

Whether aided by poltergeist activity or not, the Bengals' good fortune was short-lived. They'd go on to lose five of their last seven to post a franchise-worst 3–13 record. Sam Wyche couldn't escape the axe this time and was promptly fired by Mike Brown two days after the season ended.

Or was he? An early Christmas Eve morning meeting between Wyche and Brown ended, perhaps fittingly, in confusion. Brown claimed Wyche had quit, but Wyche insisted he had been fired by Brown. Either way, the Bengals needed a new coach, and for the first time, it was up to Mike Brown to find one.

In retrospect, the timing of Wyche's departure may have foreshadowed what was to come. Perhaps Mike Brown would have benefited from a spiritual visit with his father that Christmas Eve, similar to Jacob Marley's after-work sit-down with Ebenezer Scrooge. Maybe Paul Brown could have enticed his son to really hunker down and examine everything around him before moving forward. Whether it was prompted by not giving Wyche one more chance or the result of the slapdash coaching search—if you could call it that—that followed, things were never quite the same for the Bengals after that.

In Mike Brown's mind, the Bengals were beginning a quick period of reevaluation and rebuilding before returning to the role of regular contender.

He had no idea how long it would actually take.

***

For the first time, the Bengals would hire a head coach without Paul Brown leading the search. Would it had gone differently if he'd still been alive? Or would Brown have been committed to giving Wyche one more chance, just as he'd done after two other last-place finishes? And might that have prevented the misery the Bengals and their fans were in store for over the next decade-plus? There's no way to know for sure.

Because the Cincinnati defense had devolved into the worst in football in 1991, most figured proven defensive coordinators would top Mike Brown's wish list. Even if not, there were plenty of qualified candidates out there who would be a good fit. The scuttlebutt among league insiders was that the Cincinnati job wouldn't be terribly appealing because the Bengals had a weak scouting department and lacked a professional-level personnel director in the front office. But still, *someone* with the proper credentials would want the job.

Promoting from within seemed out of the question. Primarily because it had a status-quo flavor to it, which isn't what you want following your worst season ever. Besides, there didn't appear to be any realistic candidates on the current coaching staff.

At least not until Mike Brown returned to the office Thursday morning.

The real problem with what happened next was the optics of it. Knowing he had a lot of work ahead of him, Mike Brown went into work early on the day after Christmas. So too did the Bengals' new wide receivers coach, a young up-and-comer named David Shula. As it happened, they both wanted to talk to each other, about the exact same thing. Brown wanted to see if Shula had any interest in interviewing for the head coaching position, and Shula wanted to see if Brown had any interest in interviewing him for the gig. You can almost picture them running into each other by the copy machine, breathlessly murmuring, "Oh—I was just looking for you," as if a rom-com meet-cute.

They spent the rest of the day talking, and, the following morning, David Shula was introduced as the new head coach of the Cincinnati Bengals. The Bengals' first post-Paul Brown coaching search had lasted less than forty-eight hours—counting Christmas Day.

Keep in mind, if Mike Brown is to be believed, he hadn't even considered the possibility of replacing Sam Wyche until Wyche abruptly "quit" during their Christmas Eve coffee klatch. So you really can't give him the benefit of the doubt that he'd been mulling over coaching candidates and narrowing down the field over the last few weeks of the Bengals' flaming oil well of a season.

By all appearances, the coaching search began on December 26 when Mike Brown hung up his coat and ended when he found David Shula by the water cooler. As if Mike Brown were walking through the halls thinking, *I need to find a coach*, then saw David Shula and thought, *Ah—here's one.*

But that was just how it looked, especially in retrospect. Surely Mike Brown put much more thought into it to justify hiring the youngest coach in the history of the NFL after interviewing a grand total of zero other candidates. Not that there were many to choose from. After all, that year, the only qualified assistant jumping into a head coaching position was Dennis Green, eventually hired by Minnesota. Well, and Mike Holmgren in Green Bay. It's also easy to forget Bill Cowher—having just missed out on the Browns job—who landed in Pittsburgh. And not to rub it in, but former New York Giants coach Bill Parcells had been out of football for a year and was already starting to get the itch again. He'd return to the sidelines the following year and promptly turn the hapless New England Patriots into a Super Bowl team. Four outstanding candidates who would go on to outstanding achievements over the next decade—none of whom Mike Brown felt were worth his time.

To be fair (if that's the right word), it's unlikely any of those guys would even have been interested in the Bengals job. But it rings odd, even all these years later, that Mike Brown didn't at least give one of them (or literally anyone else, for that matter) a whirl before promoting a coach who—it's worth noting—himself wasn't on the short list for any of the other vacancies around the NFL.

On the other hand, maybe Mike Brown knew exactly what he was doing. It's more likely that he would have wanted absolutely nothing to do with a blue-chip assistant coach or a Big Tuna like Parcells stepping back into the game. Any of those options would have demanded a) more money and b) more control. Shula was a relative bargain and, being both the youngest and most surprising head coach in the NFL, was in no position to negotiate any real authority away from Mike Brown.

What is certain is that in Mike Brown's first "coaching search," he settled on a name—if not a person—familiar to football fans everywhere. And pulled a page out of Art Modell's playbook at the same time.

Like Bill Belichick, David Shula was billed as a young, budding genius, essentially pro football's Doogie Howser. Which was the only way Mike Brown could justify hiring a thirty-two-year-old for the position. While he'd be the youngest coach in NFL history—younger than several of his players, in fact—Shula came from unquestionably good pedigree. The son of legendary Miami Dolphins coach Don Shula, he'd spent seven seasons as an offensive assistant for his father, then as Jimmy Johnson's first offensive coordinator in Dallas. Which sounded great until you discovered that Johnson demoted Shula twice during his bumpy and short tenure with the Cowboys. After the second, Shula jumped to Cincinnati as wide receivers coach—a unit that was not exactly the Bengals' strong suit in 1991.

Eleven months after being demoted for the second time by a coach on the brink of becoming known as the best in the NFL, David Shula became a head coach. Most agreed that Shula was a good coach with a lot of potential. It just seemed like he hadn't yet earned the shot he was getting. Some wondered if maybe Mike Brown was basing his judgment on hope rather than reality. Or—some amateur psychologists posited— if he looked at the young coach trying to carve out his own niche in the overwhelming shadow of his legendary father and saw himself. "I guess it's up to David," Brown said in a prescient comment that takes on added meaning if you subscribe to the projection theory, "to prove how smart I am."

Before we get to reality setting in, let's give Mike Brown credit. For nearly three full weeks in the fall of 1992, he did indeed look like a genius. The Bengals' defense, which ranked dead last in the NFL the year before, smothered the Seattle Seahawks in the Kingdome on opening day, and Cincinnati cruised to a surprising 21–3 victory. A dramatic overtime win over the Los Angeles Raiders at Riverfront a week later pushed the Bengals to 2–0 for the first time in four years, and it appeared that Shula had instantly righted the Cincinnati ship.

Things looked even better a week later, when the Bengals took a 17–3 lead into the fourth quarter at Lambeau Field. With the Green

Bay Packers looking dazed and confused after starting quarterback Don Majkowski went down with an injury early in the game, the Bengals appeared well on their way to a third straight win. Led by their unheard-of backup quarterback—a "second-year obscurity," the *Cincinnati Enquirer* would label him the next day—the Packers hung around in the fourth quarter. But each time they scored, the Bengals answered to keep them at arm's length. They took a ten-point lead at the eight-minute mark and then kicked an insurance field goal to make it 23–17 with just over a minute left. The Packers regained possession at their own eight, out of time-outs with all their hopes riding on their second-year obscurity.

Little did the Bengals know that a new chapter in football history was about to begin, at their expense. Green Bay's unknown backup quarterback, cut by Atlanta after throwing just four passes as a rookie the year before, coolly led his team down the field and delivered an incredible come-from-behind victory with a thirty-five-yard touchdown pass with thirteen seconds remaining.

The Bengals had somehow lost a game they'd all but won, and the second-year obscurity soon to be known as Brett Favre had notched his first of what would become twenty-eight fourth-quarter comebacks with his first of forty-three game-winning drives.

Not surprisingly, after a loss like that, the Bengals couldn't recover. "Welcome back to reality," *Enquirer* columnist Tim Sullivan mourned on Monday morning. And reality hit like Apollo Creed upon its return. Favre's proverbial NFL bar mitzvah was the beginning of a five-game Cincinnati losing streak that consisted of lopsided losses reminiscent of the eight-game skid the year before. As the once-promising season sloshed into November, the only thing that could provide the Bengals with some relief was their upstate stepbrothers.

The Browns had managed to pick up where they'd left off the previous year, combining a handful of methodical, uninspiring victories with a bouquet of depressing defeats that balanced out into a mediocre season. A modest three-game October win streak had atoned for a 1–3 start, and a win over the flailing Bengals would have pushed the Browns into second place in the AFC Central Division at the season's midpoint. Instead, with the teams once again apparently heading in opposite directions, it was the Bengals that prevailed easily, cruising to a 30–10 victory at Riverfront. It was a satisfying moment for Shula's Bengals in a season that had begun to glide off the rails. And yet would also mark Cincinnati's final win over the Browns for nearly seven years.

So it went for the remainder of the season for both teams: the Browns meandering to within the cusp of playoff contention, then losing their final three games; the Bengals dropping six of their last seven to clinch back-to-back losing records for the first time in twelve years. At the time, it was an uncharacteristically dark period for Ohio pro football. But soon these types of seasons would become business as usual.

Both teams looked to begin new eras in 1993 and, perhaps appropriately, opened the season facing each other for the first time in sixteen years. The Bengals' David Shula Era entered its first subset with the beginning of the David Klingler Era. The year before, they'd stunned all of football by selecting Klingler with the sixth overall pick, days after saying they couldn't afford to consider taking Klingler with their myriad defensive needs. Expected to pick cornerback Troy Vincent—who would go on to play in five Pro Bowls—the Bengals surprised everyone and took Klingler, who was projected by many as a late first-round pick. Appropriately summarizing the view of the rest of creation, even Klingler's agent called the Bengals' decision "mind-boggling."

You could almost sense that Paul Brown—though not physically present to express his opinion—was the most surprised of all. Even in his final months as he battled illness, he'd warned his sons against this very thing. "Don't draft Klingler," he'd told them, even as the quarterback's popularity began to swell. "He will never make the big scene." Once again, Paul Brown was right and his progeny was wrong.

For better or worse, a year later, Klingler would take the reins after longtime fan favorite Boomer Esiason was traded to the Jets. After four uninspiring starts in 1992—including a ten-sack debut in Pittsburgh and a blowout loss in Cleveland—Klingler was now the full-time starting quarterback.

Just like the year before, things started marvelously for the Bengals. Touchdowns on their first two possessions of the new season gave them a startling 14–0 lead over the shell-shocked Browns. Once again, however, the euphoria was short-lived. The Browns clawed back to tie the game at the half, then gradually pulled away in the second, securing victory when they symbolically ran back a Klingler fumble for the game-clinching touchdown.

And with that, the Bengals were off to the races.

Nine more losses followed as they staggered to a franchise-worst 0–10 record. This time, even the Browns couldn't snap a long Cincinnati losing streak, taking care of business at Riverfront in mid-October to complete their first season sweep of the Bengals in six years. When the dust settled, Cincinnati had finished 3–13 for the second time in three seasons. And yet in some ways, they appeared to have more stability within their franchise than the Browns did.

On paper, nothing had changed for the Browns in 1993. They finished with the identical 7–9 record they'd posted in 1992, but with much more turbulence. And a Shakespearean subplot.

Things started with a flourish. Following their comeback victory over the Bengals on opening day, the Browns delivered a rousing win over the powerhouse San Francisco 49ers on *Monday Night Football*, then rallied from a 16–3 deficit in the final minutes in Los Angeles to stun the Raiders on a game-winning Eric Metcalf touchdown run with two seconds remaining. Now 3–0 for the first time in fourteen years, Belichick's Browns appeared to have arrived. But their grumpy third-year coach had already begun tugging on the thread that would eventually unravel the entire sweater.

Quarterback Bernie Kosar, a hometown hero and fan favorite since his arrival eight years before, was beginning to show the wear of several years of injuries, poor protection, and little offensive support. Never mobile or terribly athletic, Kosar's awkwardness had now become a liability, in Belichick's eyes at least, limiting what the offense could do. And since Belichick had never thought it necessary to hire an offensive coordinator, he was much more involved in the offensive play calling than a defensive-minded head coach ever should have been. Thus, the tension grew between the dictatorial coach and the entrenched quarterback. "From a distance, it appeared almost as if the quarterback and head coach took turns defying one another," *Plain Dealer* reporter Tony Grossi wrote. "Belichick calling plays that brought out the worst in Kosar, and Kosar executing with the self-defeating attitude that they would not work."

Kosar was benched in the second half in Los Angeles, and newly acquired backup Vinny Testaverde had led the miraculous comeback. Kosar returned to the helm to start the following two games but was replaced by Testaverde each time following subpar performances that led to Cleveland defeats. For their Week Seven contest in Cincinnati against the winless Bengals, Testaverde got his first start in a Browns uniform and directed an efficient 28–17 victory. Belichick had his quarterback, and it appeared Bernie would remain on the bench.

Yet in the final minutes of a dramatic victory over Pittsburgh the following week, Testaverde left the game with a separated shoulder that would keep him sidelined for six weeks. Reluctantly, Belichick turned back to Kosar, who once again was disappointing in the next game, a lethargic loss to Denver. Still, at 5–3, the Browns were in first place and poised to make a playoff run for the first time in four years. Then Bill Belichick made one of the most puzzling decisions in franchise history— one that eerily mirrored another made by Art Modell thirty years before.

Reportedly fed up with Kosar's backchat and his tendency to audible Belichick's play calls at the line of scrimmage, the following day, the coach released arguably the most popular player in Cleveland Browns history. Never mind that Testaverde, his newly ordained starting quarterback, wouldn't be able to play for another month, and that all he had left in the cupboard was obscure third-stringer Todd Philcox. Bill Belichick, like Modell back in 1963, wanted to make a point. And, just as was the case with Paul Brown three decades before, Bernie Kosar—who'd just signed a contract extension, by the way—was unceremoniously shown the door, with Art Modell's after-the-fact justification of "diminishing skills" echoing like footfalls in a marble hallway.

What followed over the next eight weeks was one of the most bizarre story lines in NFL history. Poor Todd Philcox, thrust into an impossible situation, fumbled his very first snap in his first game as starter, and it was returned for a touchdown in a display of irony too powerful to ignore. It served as the bellwether for what became a four-game losing streak and a string of six losses in seven weeks that took the Browns out of contention. Belichick had successfully sabotaged an otherwise promising season and continued to grumble and mumble through interviews. More telling, the wunderkind had now delivered his third-straight losing campaign, having devolved into, as one Cleveland writer described, "a control freak who was out of control." Throwing gasoline on the fire, Modell promptly rewarded Belichick with a two-year contract extension. Fans seethed.

Meanwhile, Kosar was picked up by the defending world-champion Dallas Cowboys as a backup and immediately made an impact. He filled in nicely for injured starter Troy Aikman and helped deliver a key divisional victory six days after being cut by the Browns. Meanwhile, Cleveland home games became vitriolic and hostile, with fans wearing Kosar Cowboys jerseys and Bernie masks, booing Belichick and every poor decision his team made as it circled the drain. It was a sweaty, ugly time that would define Belichick's career in Cleveland.

When the season was finally over, Belichick had done something no other Browns coach had done before: he'd somehow turned Cleveland against the Browns. Home attendance had dipped dramatically as the 1993 season limped toward its miserable conclusion, and the downturn would carry into the following year. Which began, appropriately, just as 1993 had: with a win over the Bengals that would send Cincinnati corkscrewing into another terrible season.

Not that there was much optimism for the 1994 Bengals, but permitting both a punt and a kickoff return for a touchdown in the first half on opening day pretty well set the tone for another Category 5 disaster season. The special teams letdowns paved the way to a Week One loss, followed by seven more, and for the third time in four years since Paul Brown's death, the Bengals stood winless at the season's midpoint. The highlight of the season—if you could call it that—was a memorable Week Nine affair at Riverfront against the world-champion Dallas Cowboys. With obscure third-string quarterback Jeff Blake making his first NFL start, the hapless Bengals grabbed a 14–0 lead over the 6–1 Cowboys and fought to the bitter end, eventually falling by just three points.

Blake's sudden ascendancy—he would start each of the remaining seven games—ended the Klingler era after a year and a half and helped the Bengals "rally" for a second straight 3–13 mark that earned them the fifth pick in the draft. The following April, they traded up to the No. 1 spot to select a special player that appeared capable of turning things around.

Ki-Jana Carter had lit up the world as a Penn State running back. In his final season, he rushed for more than 1,500 yards and twenty-three touchdowns while averaging an astonishing 7.8 yards per carry as he led the Nittany Lions to a national championship. An Ohio native, he'd be returning home to a franchise desperate for a star and signed a seven-year, $19 million contract that made him the highest-paid rookie in NFL history.

What happened next—and more appropriately, how it happened—made even the most practical of Bengals fans wonder if their team was indeed haunted.

On his third carry of his first preseason game that August, Carter tore the anterior cruciate ligament in his left knee, requiring major recon-structive surgery, and was lost for his entire rookie season. Four minutes in, the Ki-Jana Carter Era became an instant tragedy. Asked to rank the disappointment on a scale of one to ten, Mike Brown gave it a ten. David Shula called it a nightmare. "It's probably one of the worst days of my life," an emotional Carter said the following day when his diagnosis became official. He would return the following year and played four seasons for the Bengals, primarily as a backup, but never became the player everyone had hoped for.

Players often get injured in sports, and many times highly touted rookies don't pan out. But rarely—if ever—had there been such a stark example of bad luck than the No. 1 pick in the NFL draft—a player the Bengals had traded away their two top picks to select—seeing his career derailed on the third play of his first game. First *exhibition* game, at that.

Despite the emotional body blow, the 1995 Bengals actually put together their finest season in five years. They avoided the crippling starts of the previous two seasons by winning their first two games and stayed on their feet despite a four-game losing streak. They even had a chance to finish with a .500 record before a trip to Cleveland in Week Sixteen—for perhaps the most surreal game in NFL history.

***

Paul Brown tried to warn us.

Long before he died, long before Art Modell suddenly and starkly ripped up stakes and dragged the beloved Browns out of Cleveland, Paul Brown recognized Art Modell for exactly what he was.

"The relationship between the two of us has been described as a personality conflict," Brown wrote in his 1979 autobiography, "but it was much more than that. It was basic conflict between two different styles and two different styles of operating—one from knowledge and experience, the other from a complete lack of either."

Paul Brown had been dead four years on the sunshiny November afternoon in Baltimore when Modell proclaimed he had no choice but to move the Browns from Cleveland. But it's not hard to imagine Brown looking over that callous display while shaking his head and saying, "I told you so."

He knew before most that Modell was all about business and much less so—if at all—about football. That isn't all that unusual for the owner of a professional sports team. But moving one of the most entrenched and revered franchises as a result of impatience and jealousy rather than logic or justification required a unique brand of deviousness. And at the end of the day, it wasn't so much what he did, but how he did it, that earned him a spot in the double-dealing hall of fame.

Amazingly, for a year that would end with Cleveland down a football team, 1995 began as what appeared would be the dawn of a new, golden era for the Browns. On New Year's Day, they won their first playoff game in five years, defeating the New England Patriots before a sold-out crowd at Cleveland Stadium. It proved to be the cap on a season that was—if not exactly exciting—at least satisfying and somewhat healing.

Like buttered toast to an upset stomach, the 1994 Browns soothed the acid reflux from the BernieGate scandal of the year before. With Vinny Testaverde now ensconced as the starting quarterback, he led a low-risk, low-reward offense that provided just enough to get the job done. The backbone of the team was a stellar defense—under the direction of a then-unknown coordinator named Nick Saban—that simply stymied opponents, limiting them to less than twenty points in thirteen of sixteen games and to single digits six times. The Browns roared to a 6–1 start that included a second-straight season sweep of the winless Bengals, then reached 8–2 and stood alone in first place in the AFC Central in mid-November. Things soured down the stretch as they were overtaken and overwhelmed by a gritty Pittsburgh team that simply had the Browns' number, stumping them three times, including a playoff blowout. Still, the Browns' 11–5 record was their best in eight years, and it appeared they'd finally evolved into a contender under the still-not-quite-trusted Bill Belichick.

Hopes were high for 1995, particularly when Modell landed star free agent wide receiver Andre Rison. Suddenly, an offense that had been efficient at best now included one of the greatest playmakers in football. The expectations spilled well outside of the 216 area code, with *Sports Illustrated* driving the bandwagon, picking the Browns to make it to the Super Bowl. Which, in many cases, by itself represents the smooch-a-roo of doom.

The Rison signing was the primary reason for the excitement, but in reality, it was one of the worst decisions Modell had ever made. Put simply, if you believe everything he would later say about his dire financial straits, he absolutely couldn't afford Rison and knew it, literally borrowing money to pay Rison's signing bonus. But like an addicted gambler (or, more likely, a terrible businessman), he went all-in, going against the odds in the hopes of the biggest payday of his life. And in a roundabout way, it worked.

For a month, things looked good. The Browns won three of their first four, including an impressive win over a strong Kansas City Chiefs team that wound up posting a 13–3 record. But there were ominous signs that it was all an illusion. Even in victory, the powerful defense—now without Saban, who had departed for Michigan State—that had propelled the team the year before suddenly looked suspect, and playmaker Rison had caught a grand total of nine passes in four games. The bubble burst in October, as the Browns lost three straight, bottoming out with a logic-defying home loss to the expansion Jacksonville Jaguars.

In utter desperation, Belichick benched Testaverde—who in fact was enjoying the finest statistical season of his career—in favor of rookie Eric Zeier for a win-or-else contest in Cincinnati. Two days before Halloween, the Browns pulled another trick-or-treat prank on their fans, falsely suggesting they'd both righted the ship and found their next great quarterback. In his first start, Zeier looked like Otto Graham, throwing for better than 300 yards. His primary target was—surprise,

surprise—Andre Rison, who caught seven passes for a whopping 173 yards. After surging to a ten-point lead with three minutes left, the Browns watched a frantic Bengals rally—led by ostracized David Klingler—wipe out the deficit and force overtime. But a Cleveland interception in sudden-death set up the game-winning field goal, and the Browns had snapped their inexplicable losing streak. Little did they know it would be the franchise's last "normal" game.

That's because by the following Sunday, word had leaked: Art Modell was renting himself a U-Haul. The Browns were off to Baltimore, for reasons beyond the comprehension of anyone who didn't own an NFL team.

At the heart of Modell's justification was rickety old Cleveland Stadium. There was no argument that the then-sixty-four-year-old ballpark was falling apart and needed, at the very least, a dramatic overhaul to be a sustainable NFL venue. Modell had stepped in to help the city in the 1970s by purchasing the toilet-seat-shaped money pit and overseeing its operations. Now he watched his tenants, the baseball Indians, get a brand-new ballpark in 1994, while that fall the NBA's Cavaliers got a sparkling arena they really didn't need or ask for. Told to be patient, Modell waited his turn.

Which he'd also been told before. He was ready to build a new stadium in the suburbs in the mid-1970s. The city pleaded with him not to, explaining that it would kill its efforts to revitalize a downtown that looked postapocalyptic. So he stayed. In 1984, a plan to fund a multipurpose domed stadium appeared on the Cuyahoga County ballot and was soundly defeated. Five years later, Modell led a charge for renovating the stadium but was told that a baseball-only ballpark was the priority. Once again, Modell was asked to take a seat. Once Gateway—the aptly named initiative that eventually built Jacobs Field and Gund Arena—was taken care of, the city would figure out what to do with Cleveland Stadium. Modell even participated in the campaign to whip up public support for Gateway, which narrowly passed in the spring of 1990.

Once the funding was set up and construction on Jacobs Field and Gund Arena began, Modell turned to city officials like an employee meeting with his boss about a long-overdue raise. Modell was told now wasn't a great time and to hang in there—they'd get to his problem eventually. Now Modell, not only as a jealous owner but as a landlord who'd just lost a tenant, was genuinely irritated. "They spent $650 million for a baseball park, a basketball arena, a rock and roll museum, and a science museum," he later said, "and all I wanted was indoor plumbing."

For the next couple years, they dickered, with Modell expressing his frustrations in the media, albeit mildly. While reporters naturally concluded that the Browns might skip town if a deal ultimately couldn't be struck, Modell never hinted at a nuclear option. He denied that he was thinking about moving or that he ever even considered the possibility. He did say he'd never move the team as long as his family owned it but said he might be forced to sell it to someone who would. During one flurry of rumors in 1982, Modell put his commitment to the city in dramatic terms: "I guess I'm going to have to go out to Public Square, strip down to my underwear, and pledge undying loyalty to Moses Cleaveland to convince people I'm not leaving." With statements (and disturbing visual images) like that coming at regular intervals over the years, the city understandably believed him.

They also believed him just before the 1995 season began, when Modell said he was calling off any and all discussions about the stadium so the focus could turn to what was happening on the field. And, just when everyone agreed to his suggestion to take a break from negotiations, Modell started seriously talking to Baltimore about moving the Browns there.

It's fair to conclude the city didn't take things quite seriously enough quite fast enough. On the other hand, they'd just spent $400 million of the taxpayers' money for two new sports construction projects. The timing of promising another multimillion-dollar boondoggle had to be carefully considered, especially for as narrow as Gateway's electoral margin had been. And remember, the moment Modell wanted to cash in was arguably the lowest-ever ebb of the Browns' popularity, coinciding with the deep-space-cold administration of Bill Belichick.

But it wasn't as if the city were totally ignoring the problem. County commissioners placed an extension of the same funding structure that built Jacobs Field and Gund Arena on the ballot in November of 1995 to pay for $154 million in improvements to Cleveland Stadium. Throughout the fall, even with Modell's moratorium in effect, the drums started beating—if the initiative didn't pass on November 7, the Browns might bail.

Modell would later say that the money was only about half of what was needed to truly renovate Cleveland Stadium. But he never said this in the weeks leading up to the election. Everyone was talking about how important the approval of the tax extension was to keeping the Browns in Cleveland and how the vote would give a good indication of what the future might hold. Little did anyone know that Modell didn't care. He was already negotiating with Baltimore and signed the agreement to move the team eleven days before the election. As it turned out, the secret lasted less than a week, but Modell was fully prepared to allow Cuyahoga County to vote on—and potentially pass—a funding issue to renovate a stadium that would have no team to play in it.

As much as Clevelanders will always hate to hear it, Modell had some valid complaints. Whether or not they were enough to justify moving the team, when and how he did is highly debatable. The city seemed to be counting on the idea that Modell hadn't moved the Browns before, so he wouldn't move them now. And since Modell had never directly threatened to move the team and never clearly articulated his demands, their approach was understandable. It turned out Modell was more committed to moving than anyone thought. He just decided not to say so until he did it.

However slow the city may have been to take action, Modell wound up looking like Snidely Whiplash. The city had provided him an opportunity to get most of the funding he'd need. Had Modell come out and publicly said it wasn't going to be enough or that he now wanted a new stadium rather than renovations to the old one, it might have prompted another solution or at least an honest negotiation with all the cards on the table. But he said nothing, and during his own moratorium, he signed a deal with Baltimore—then complained that Cleveland wouldn't talk to him. In football terms, he'd called time out, then picked up the ball and ran into the end zone while everybody was on the sideline.

(Adding some intrigue was a bombshell plot twist shortly after Modell's death seventeen years later. A pair of local politicians revealed that Modell *had* been offered a chance to be a part of the Gateway project as it was being put together. He was approached with a proposal that would expand the funding to include a new stadium for the Browns just south of where Jacobs Field would be. But, they said, for reasons that still remain a mystery, Modell declined. Out of respect for their friendship with Modell, the pair remained silent for years, even as he railed against the city for failing to cooperate. A Modell family spokesman insisted the story wasn't true, that the city told Modell they'd take care of him and Cleveland Stadium later, after Gateway was in motion. Thus, this anecdote becomes the grassy-knoll shooter of the Browns' move.)

In retrospect, it was clear Modell was eventually going to get what he wanted—and would have gotten it had he played square. Twenty-four hours after the move was announced, the stadium funding issue passed in a landslide with 75 percent of the vote, and the city quickly whipped up a lucrative counteroffer to keep the Browns in Cleveland. Modell shrugged it off, saying it was too little, too late. Which, for the ballot issue at least, he could have said two months earlier. Without saying so, Modell came to the conclusion that a solution wasn't possible—essentially calling off the negotiation process before it truly began.

Did the city blow it by overestimating Modell's loyalty? To some extent, probably.

Did Modell ultimately act like a weapons-grade weasel? Definitely.

Even Baltimore—"where the league's soul first started leaking," *Cincinnati Enquirer* columnist Tim Sullivan opined—felt a little icky about the whole thing. With the move of the Baltimore Colts to Indianapolis eleven years earlier still fresh in everyone's mind, many criticized Modell for how he handled the situation. "We've got blood on our hands," one columnist wrote in the *Baltimore Sun*.

The debate over how justified Modell truly was will rage on forever, but then and now, it's essentially moot. On November 6, 1995, Modell announced he was moving the Browns to Baltimore. The legacy Paul Brown had created was being ripped out of Cleveland and moved to just a few miles away from where Brown's coaching career began in Maryland at tiny Severn Prep. The news rocked the NFL but particularly shook the Bengals franchise, which was deeply connected to the Browns. "Cleveland is the branch from which we sprung," Mike Brown said the day the move was announced.

Now a dead team walking, the Browns' Super Bowl aspirations of just a few weeks before seemed like a Tolkienesque fantasy. Crippled by a lack of emotion and cohesion, the Browns staggered to six straight losses, with each home game feeling like an amalgamation of a heinous murder trial and a tragic funeral. The story that had begun in Cleveland in September 1946 with Paul Brown on the sideline would come to a conclusion on December 17, 1995, at the same place—fittingly, against the other team that Paul Brown created.

It only seemed right that the Bengals would be the final team to visit Cleveland Municipal Stadium, just a few weeks after the twenty-fifth anniversary of their initial trip there. With all advertising and sponsorship stripped from billboards and signage inside the stadium, an emotional crowd filtered in. Many fans brought tools with them, with which they would remove seats and other souvenirs. The game itself was an afterthought, since most expected it to follow the script of the previous six displays of debacle the lifeless Browns had provided.

Instead, the Browns emerged from the doldrums and looked like a genuine football team for the first time in two months. Behind the determined running of star-crossed tailback Earnest Byner, the Browns dominated an improved Bengals team and cruised to a 26–10 victory. After the clock hit zero, a handful of Browns players took a lap around the stadium, high-fiving and embracing tearful fans not in triumph, but in sorrow.

An era was over. The team Paul Brown had, if not created, then molded into reality, was dead.

***

You may think you've seen what a four-alarm pro sports dumpster fire looks like. But there's no way it could be worse than the hellscape that nearly unfolded in Cleveland after the Browns move was announced.

The Browns' twenty-five-year lease agreement with Cleveland signed in 1974 wasn't set to expire until after the 1998 season. For all the pomp and circumstance surrounding Modell's announcement, technically and legally, he couldn't just up and move the team. The city was lawyered up and pissed off.

Like a spurned spouse in an ugly divorce, in the weeks that followed,

Cleveland was fully prepared to stick it to Modell, even at its own expense. *You can move the team if you want,* the city essentially told him, *but we're holding you to your lease.* To which Modell basically responded: *Okay, fuckers. Let's dance.*

So picture—if you can—what would have followed. Modell would have gone ahead and moved the team. Each week, the Browns would have practiced in Baltimore, then flown to Cleveland to play its home games before small and either hostile or apathetic crowds. Adding to the fun, Modell revealed that, under these conditions, he'd strip the team of whatever talent it had and simply stock up draft picks in anticipation of finally playing its games in Baltimore in 1999. Best of all, Modell would keep the despised Bill Belichick as head coach throughout the fiasco, just to twist the knife into Cleveland's solar plexus a little deeper.

Good times. Three years of them, in fact.

Clearly, the NFL wanted to avoid this particular kind of pissing match, what commissioner Paul Tagliabue said would have been the "Super Bowl of litigation." Taking Cleveland Mayor Michael White and civic leaders aside, the league talked them down, explaining how while this course of action might feel good and indeed hurt and embarrass Modell, it would also ultimately prevent Cleveland from getting another team. White & Co., who'd publicly pledged to fight to the bitter end, listened.

A compromise was reached. Cleveland agreed to drop its lawsuit to force Modell and the Browns to stay, and the league assured Cleveland that it would have an NFL team no later than 1999. The name "Browns" and the team colors would remain in Cleveland, and the league would even float some of the cash to pay for the new stadium until the new owner—not the city—could pay it back. "Cleveland got a a hell of a deal—a hell of a deal," Modell said. "If I had gotten half of that deal a year ago, I'd have stayed in Cleveland. That's how outrageous it is."

Whatever sour grapes Modell might have had were temporary. He was now free and clear to take his team to Baltimore. His first course of action? Promptly firing Bill Belichick, which he did five days later, on Valentine's Day—an ironic end to one of the ugliest and most damaging sports relationships ever.

A greasy public relations nightmare for the NFL had been neatly avoided. But often forgotten in the triumphant glow of the Browns' eventual rebirth as an expansion team in 1999 was that there was a time when it appeared the new Browns wouldn't have been new.

The NFL, understandably hesitant to provide a token expansion franchise in a time when expansion wasn't optimal (and swell its membership to an uneven thirty-one teams), toyed with the notion of relocating an existing, financially struggling franchise to Cleveland and killing two birds with one stone.

There were several rumored possible candidates, with nearly half of the NFL looking to cash in on new stadium deals in the aftermath of a whopping four franchise moves in 1995 alone. The first potential candidate to replace the Browns was the long-suffering Tampa Bay Buccaneers, who'd never really connected with their Gulf Coast audience.

The other? You guessed it: the Cincinnati Bengals.

Just days after Art Modell announced the Browns were skipping town, WBAL in Baltimore—which had been the first outlet to break the news of the Browns' move—reported that the NFL was considering a truly bizarre solution to the problem.

As the story goes, the league was considering moving the Bengals to Cleveland, where they'd assume the name and colors of the Browns. And it got even crazier: the team that Modell was taking to Baltimore would be renamed the Baltimore Bengals.

Just sit with that for a second.

Strange as it may have seemed, there was a logic to it. At the time, Cleveland was the thirteenth-largest television market in the US, Baltimore No. 22, and Cincinnati No. 30. The Browns generally drew almost twice as many fans to their games as the Bengals, who hadn't been a contender for years and had struggled to draw both ticket buyers and television viewers.

As bugnuts as that particular plot twist would have been, in a bizarre way, it would have been appropriate. Already intertwined in so many ways, the Browns and Bengals would finally have become a single entity, as Paul Brown's two legacies would have become one. Mike Brown would have followed his father's footsteps to Northeast Ohio. And Art

Modell would have wound up with a team represented by a name personally selected by his bitter rival. The Count of Monte Cristo couldn't have orchestrated revenge any better.

The Bengals-to-Cleveland story was immediately denied, primarily on the grounds that Brown wanted to wait until the following March, when Hamilton County voters would decide whether to flip the bill on a new stadium for the Bengals. But in actuality, the idea of the "Baltimore Bengals" had originally come from Mike Brown himself.

Believe it or not, Paul Brown had started complaining about his stadium before Art Modell did. Brown first sniveled about revenue problems at Riverfront in 1982—when the ballpark was just twelve years old—and Mike Brown picked up the torch shortly after his father's death: Riverfront Stadium was hopelessly inadequate, the Bengals weren't getting much of the gameday revenue, without a new stadium and financial structure the Bengals might as well curl up and die. Et cetera, et cetera.

At that point, in 1993, five cities had just gone through the rigorous (and expensive) process of attempting to land an expansion NFL franchise. After the league selected Jacksonville and Charlotte, that left Memphis, St. Louis, and—wait for it—Baltimore on the outside looking in. In early 1995, Brown stated he would negotiate with those cities, setting a firm deadline for the city of Cincinnati to come up with a stadium financing plan to present to the voters. In the meantime, that summer he visited Baltimore and had some long conversations with city officials, who offered him essentially the same deal Modell would get.

Back in Cincinnati, the city made the deadline, literally, by two minutes. When Brown was told the news, he had already drafted a press statement saying farewell to Cincinnati. And in his coat pocket was a plane ticket to Baltimore.

The Bengals would stay in Cincinnati at least long enough to see if the voters were willing to pay for a new stadium. In the meantime—perhaps to Mike Brown's dismay—Art Modell grabbed one of the empty chairs before the music stopped by taking the deal Brown left on the table with the crab cakes.

But even in losing a desperate suitor in Baltimore, Brown was able to cash in on Modell's move almost as much as Modell did himself. With the Browns' move so prominent (along with the Los Angeles Rams' shift to St. Louis, the Houston Oilers' to Nashville, and the Raiders' return to Oakland), Hamilton County officials were desperate to not have Cincinnati become the latest former NFL city. Voters knew that if the Browns could leave Cleveland, the Bengals could (and would) absolutely tap out of Cincinnati.

On the Hamilton County ballot in March of 1996 was Issue 1, which would raise the county sales tax by a half percent for twenty years to pay for new stadiums for the Bengals and Reds. Voters were promised an annual property tax rebate (later revoked) and that the city would provide extra money to Cincinnati's public schools (deferred for years). And there was no subtlety involved. Mike Brown made it crystal clear: you vote this down, we're outta here—almost certainly to Cleveland. "No one likes new taxes, and few of us are favorably disposed to extortion," *Enquirer* columnist Tim Sullivan wrote. "Yet the idea of the Cincinnati Bengals moving—and to Cleveland of all places—was more than most Cincinnatians could stomach."

Less an election than a hostage situation, Issue 1 passed in a landslide. Hamilton County handed Mike Brown a briefcase full of money, and he pulled the bound-and-gagged Bengals out of his trunk. Thanks, in large part, to Art Modell.

Cincinnati breathed a sigh of relief. Then, very quickly, some intense buyer's remorse began to settle in.

It was, the *Wall Street Journal* would later declare, "one of the worst professional sports deals ever struck by a local government." Hamilton County paid for nearly all of the new stadium, with no financial assistance from surrounding counties, the team, or the NFL. Sure, the new ballpark would make Riverfront look like a yurt, but at what cost? The Bengals' lease terms were laughably favorable and only got more ridiculous over the duration of the lease. Ten years after it opened, the cost of simply operating the stadium amounted to better than 16 percent of the county's annual budget. Over the years, funding for several other county programs was slashed to pay for the Bengals' new lair.

To be fair, it wasn't just Cincinnati that got rooked. Many of the new stadium deals ginned up in the aftermath of the rash of mid-1990s moves were increasingly lucrative for the teams and buried local governments in debt. But none was worse than Cincinnati's. Art Modell's moving the

Browns didn't cost Cincinnati its team, but it did cost it a lot. Originally budgeted at $170 million, the Bengals' new stadium wound up costing an incredible $453 million, becoming the most expensive public works project in the history of the city.

Ironically, Cleveland's misfortune actually helped the Bengals stay put, albeit at an astronomical price. Had Modell not moved the Browns, Mike Brown may not have had the leverage he needed to hornswoggle voters into a new stadium, and the Bengals might have been the ones who moved to Baltimore. Then Cincinnati, not Cleveland, would have been the city panhandling for an expansion team. So while Mike Brown didn't move his team as Modell did, it's fair to ask if he orchestrated just as much civic and financial damage.

Over his long career, Paul Brown had proven to be an incredibly astute and calculating businessman. But it's difficult to imagine him involved in anything as deceitful as what his two teams did to their home cities.

***

With a bright new future on the way symbolized by architectural plans for a glimmering new stadium, the Bengals closed out the decade in the same sorry shape they'd started it.

The 1996 season saw the Bengals begin a tradition of false promise they'd master over the next few years. They once again started the year miserably, losing six of their first seven games. After watching his team blow a 21–0 lead to lose in the final minutes in San Francisco in late October, Mike Brown axed coach David Shula, who'd somehow survived long enough to compile a stunningly terrible 19–52 record over five seasons. For all the high promise and potential Shula had when he was hired as head coach, his primary legacy was racking up fifty losses faster than any other coach in NFL history. He never again coached in the NFL in any capacity, and stayed out of the game altogether until becoming the receivers coach at Dartmouth College—more than twenty-one years after getting fired by the Bengals.

It was a fitting bookend for the David Shula experience. Mike Brown seemed to have both hired him and fired him for misguided reasons. It

wasn't Shula's on-life-support win-loss record that bothered Brown—
"As far as I'm concerned, he has done a good job," Brown was somehow able to say without bursting into flames—but rather the logistical
requirements of building the new stadium that cost Shula his job. The
Bengals needed to sell enough personal seat licenses for the new ballpark by the following April for construction to be green-lit. And with
the beleaguered fan base weary of Shula the Boy Wonder, he had to be
let go—not necessarily to improve the team, but to spark PSL sales. To
follow along with that strategy, many expected Mike Brown to seek out a
marquee name to generate interest and hope for the franchise. But while
that approach might work, it would also require Brown to surrender
more control to the new coach—which wasn't going to happen.

The compromise was offensive coordinator Bruce Coslet—fresh
off an unremarkable turn on the dance floor as head coach of the New
York Jets—who was tapped to drag the Bengals across the finish line
and sell some PSLs. And against all logic, as if Mike Brown had scripted
it himself, Coslet instantly led the Bengals on one of the best stretches in
their history. They won seven of their last nine games—including a pair
of fourth-quarter comeback victories over the Baltimore Ravens (or, as
many really looked at them at the time, the Browns with a coat of purple
paint). The '96 Bengals closed things out with a last-minute touchdown
to defeat Indianapolis in the finale to secure an 8–8 record. It was their
first nonlosing mark in six years and seemed to indicate that the Bengals,
with Coslet at the helm and promising young talent like quarterback Jeff
Blake and receivers Darnay Scott and Carl Pickens quickly developing
into stars, had turned a corner. More important, PSL sales ticked up, and
the new stadium was officially on the way.

They picked up where they'd left off on opening day, 1997. Three
fourth-quarter touchdowns—two on Ki-Jana Carter runs—wiped out a
21–3 Arizona lead and gave the Bengals their eighth victory in their last
ten games. It seemed they were off to an exciting season that would see
them contend for or potentially return to the playoffs. Instead, they lost
their next seven games to torpedo those hopes. They then embarked on
another tantalizing late-season tease, led by a pair of fairly random dis-
coveries: the emergence of second-round draft choice Corey Dillon into
a star running back and the renaissance of quarterback Boomer Esiason.

Dillon became an overnight sensation, quite literally, when he rushed for a league-rookie-record 246 yards and four touchdowns in a Thursday night contest with the Tennessee Oilers. It represented nearly a quarter of his season total and helped push him over the thousand-yard mark. But it was experience, not youth, that really sparked the turnaround.

After nine relatively successful years in Cincinnati, Esiason was shipped off the S.S. Klingler and traded to New York, where he rejoined Coslet in 1993. After four mediocre seasons with the Jets and Cardinals, Esiason contemplated retirement but was talked into returning to Cincinnati at the age of thirty-six to back up Blake. Boomer came off the bench to clinch a victory in Indianapolis, then was named the starter two weeks later and embarked on the greatest stretch of his career. Over the final two months of the season, Esiason completed 63 percent of his passes, throwing for thirteen touchdowns and just a pair of interceptions as the Bengals won six of their last eight games to finish a respectable 7–9.

Once again, hopes were high as the season ended. But when ABC offered Esiason more money to become part of the *Monday Night Football* broadcast team than Mike Brown was offering to return to the Bengals, the '97 mojo vanished. The Bengals turned to veteran Neil O'Donnell in free agency, who, like Esiason, had just endured an unenjoyable tour with the Jets after a successful run in Pittsburgh. For all the hand-wringing about not re-signing Esiason, O'Donnell wasn't terrible, despite being sacked thirty times in eleven starts. Neither was Dillon, who mirrored his rookie season with another thousand-yard campaign. It was the Cincinnati defense that doomed the season, as a unit that had been a weakness for years devolved into an utter disaster. The 1998 Bengals allowed twenty-eight points per game, a league-worst, as opponents scored thirty-one points or more a whopping seven times—not surprisingly, all Cincinnati losses.

A comeback victory over the Steelers at Riverfront pushed the Bengals to 2–3 in mid-October, but nine straight losses would follow. They finished 3–13 for the fourth time in the eight seasons since Paul Brown's passing, and after three years of teased optimism, the Bengals were once again nowhere, finishing dead last in a crowded AFC Central Division that was about to get one more member with the return of the Bengals' intrastate counterparts.

After three years of no football and lots of hard feelings, the Cleveland Browns were ready to join the NFL.

3

I-71 Tug of War
1970–1975

After three years of baby steps and tough lessons, the Cincinnati Bengals were ready to join the NFL.

A brand-new NFL, as it happened, thanks in part to Paul Brown. After the merger with the AFL was official, a handful of owners—including Art Modell—dug in their heels about how the league would be realigned. Many of the AFL owners were fine with everybody staying put: the AFL would become the American Football Conference and the NFL teams would make up the National Football Conference. While Modell endorsed the "as-is" merger proposal, Brown went nutsy. He'd only agreed to the pit stop in the AFL because a full merger was right around the corner. This was less a merger than a corporate takeover, and Brown wouldn't stand for it. He convinced his fellow AFL owners that the pot needed to be stirred to truly cement the merger. A late counter-proposal suggested that three NFL teams would jump to the AFC to balance things out, but the old guard was still hesitant. Art Modell, for one, insisted that the Browns jumping to the AFC and abandoning the team's long-standing rivalries would, in his words, "emasculate the NFL."

The compromise—and the literal beginning of the Browns-Bengals rivalry—occurred in a Manhattan hospital room. NFL owners assembled in New York in the spring of 1969 to discuss, among other things, who would join the new conference. Perhaps exacerbated by the ongoing discussion, Modell developed a bleeding ulcer and collapsed in his hotel room. He was driven to the hospital by NFL commissioner Pete Rozelle, who kept up with the negotiations by phone.

With Rozelle, Pittsburgh owner Art Rooney, and New York Giants owner Wellington Mara gathered around his hospital bed, the hemorrhaging Modell proposed a solution, quite possibly brought on by the Schedule II narcotics flowing through his bloodstream. He'd take the Browns to the AFC, he said, but only if Mara agreed to it (in essence, killing the long-standing Browns-Giants rivalry) and if Pittsburgh would come along with the Browns to maintain that rivalry. While the Browns would lose one rivalry with the Giants, he contended they could start a new one with Paul Brown's Cincinnati Bengals, which, really, had symbolically begun long before the merger. The Browns and Steelers were placed in the new Central Division alongside Brown's Bengals and the Houston Oilers.

Thus, Modell agreed to allow the Browns to be, in his words, emasculated, abandoning the long-standing traditions of the franchise's first quarter-century to enter a bold new era—one symbolized, oddly enough, by a highway.

When the initial phase of Interstate 71 was completed (those who still use it today know that it will never quite be "finished") in the early 1970s, it became Ohio's Oregon Trail—providing a diagonal line from the state's southwest corner to its northeast corner. In essence, it connected its two biggest cities, Cincinnati and Cleveland. And the construction of the freeway mirrored the timeline of the creation of the Browns-Bengals rivalry itself: beginning in the 1960s with Brown's firing and his efforts to create the Bengals, and truly becoming reality in the early 1970s when the Bengals joined the NFL and the teams began to play each other. Just as I-71 opened for business, you could visualize the Browns and Bengals each picking up their end of the interstate and pulling with all their might—first franchise dragged past Columbus would lose.

Even more than five years after their bitter breakup in Cleveland, there remained a coldness between Modell and Brown that would certainly translate when their respective teams took the same football field. But Brown's return to coaching and the AFL/NFL merger seemed to represent a sort of glasnost for the two men. Modell had supported Brown's efforts to bring a team to Cincinnati, and he would spend the next several years going out of his way to be courteous and respectful to Brown at league meetings. He'd often go on and on with friends and colleagues about the high regard in which he held Brown.

Heading into 1970, Modell was in a good position to be sanctimonious. While his team had sacrificed several tangible benefits by jumping to the AFC, it appeared that one of the advantages was that the Browns were positioned to be a dominant force in the new conference. Looking like the lone grown-up at the kids table, the Browns were the clear favorite in the newfangled Central Division. The team that had just cruised to three straight division titles and reached the NFL Championship Game each of the two previous years was now residing in a division in which none of its three rivals had posted a winning record the year before, combining to win only eleven of their forty-two games. It was almost laughable to imagine the Oilers, Steelers, or still-expansion-label Bengals topping the Browns over the course of a season.

But even before the historic inaugural postmerger season began, the Browns got a sense of the magnitude of the new world in which they lived. The first official Browns-Bengals game was set for mid-October in Cleveland, but the rivalry would unofficially kick off with an exhibition contest on August 29, 1970, at Cincinnati's brand-new Riverfront Stadium. It turned out to be the most highly anticipated meaningless game in either team's history.

Tickets were gone two weeks before. When the Browns arrived at their downtown hotel, the lobby was adorned with football decorations, staffers were dressed as football referees, and waitresses in the hotel restaurant wore football jerseys. It was still summertime, but the game had taken on a Super Bowl feel. Reflecting the historical atmosphere, the football used for the opening kickoff was whisked away and donated to the Pro Football Hall of Fame. Before the contest, Art Modell exchanged pleasantries with Bengals president John Sawyer down on the field but, not surprisingly, never crossed paths with Paul Brown. "This intercity series between two Ohio teams is going to be bigger than either Paul or me," Modell said in an attempt to pivot away from the conspicuous non-meeting. "It will be going on long after both of us are gone."

And the game itself—hollow as it may have been in actuality—lived up to the hype. Better than 57,000 fans packed into the new ballpark, a tally that would stand for the next thirty years as the Bengals' largest preseason crowd at Riverfront Stadium. Presumably foreshadowing the dominance that was to come in the fall, the Browns jumped to a quick 14–0 lead, but Cincinnati fought back, clawing to a three-point halftime advantage. After battling through a see-saw second half, the Bengals prevailed thanks to a late touchdown pass from their reserve quarterback, who would become a much bigger character in the rivalry in the years to come: Sam Wyche.

While it was still just a preseason game, it wasn't the usual exhibition rhetoric that flowed from the locker rooms afterward. A proud Paul Brown declared that "A football team may have been born tonight" and clung to the game ball presented to him by his players. "This one, fellas," he said, "I'll keep." In that spirit, *Plain Dealer* columnist Chuck Heaton called the Bengals' victory "the magic moment Paul Brown must have been dreaming about for the past seven years." Conversely, longtime Browns offensive lineman Dick Schafrath admitted he was "ashamed and embarrassed" to lose to the Bengals, even though the Browns had mostly played their reserves in the second half.

Forty-two days later, the teams met again, this time with real stakes—in some ways equating or even surpassing the World Series, which provided an ironic parallel. Cincinnati's Reds would host the Baltimore Orioles at Riverfront for Game Two of the 1970 Fall Classic at the same time the Browns and Bengals kicked off in Cleveland. "What matter if the World Series is going on," the *Enquirer* wondered. "In Cleveland today, THE game is here . . ."

The Browns had won two of their first three games to grab a share of first place in the division, with the Bengals one game back. But more important than the impact to the standings was the cloud of history that hovered over the contest. "I've played through so many Sunday afternoons and so many games, it will just be another game," Paul Brown said drolly that week. Absolutely no one believed him. Modell, at least, couldn't help but crack a bit of a smile when he offered his own "It's just another ballgame" quote. Adding to the general disingenuousness, the coach never referred to the Browns by their name, opting instead to call them the "Clevelands." Perhaps it was out of modesty, but there seemed to be more to it than that.

It was only the second time Paul Brown had returned to Cleveland since his firing nearly eight years before. And, perhaps fittingly, he would leave controversy in his wake.

Brown met with Blanton Collier, his replacement as Browns coach, on the field before the game. Legend has it that as they chatted, Brown mentioned that win or lose, he intended to go straight to the locker room after the game rather than meeting at midfield for the traditional postgame handshake. It was an AFL tradition for the coach to leave the field with his players, and later, Brown cited a direction from the league office to try to avoid an increasing number of incidents with fans on the field after games. And, for what it's worth, the two coaches hadn't shaken hands after their preseason meeting, even though Collier had jogged out to midfield for just that purpose. In retrospect, Brown thought that Collier—who was deaf in one ear—hadn't heard his explanation.

Even without the "Return of Paul Brown" angle, the cool, overcast afternoon took on a surreal feel. With the teams' plain helmets nearly an identical shade of orange and their similar jerseys and color schemes, they looked like twins whose mother wasn't making any effort to dress them differently. In fact, many remarked that the contest looked and felt like an intrasquad game. On the contrary, it carried much more magnitude and intensity. It marked the first time a team from Cincinnati had played a team from Cleveland in a regular season game in one of the four major American pro sports leagues since the Cleveland Spiders and Cincinnati Reds had closed out the National League baseball season in October 1899. The Reds clobbered the Spiders that afternoon, 19–3, and at the outset of the revival seventy-one years later, it looked like the Bengals might follow the same script.

They hushed the mammoth crowd of 83,520 by surging to a 10–0 lead. The Browns, ten-point favorites, got on the board with a safety, when defensive end Walter Johnson sacked Cincinnati quarterback Virgil Carter in the end zone, then pulled within one point on a short Bill

Nelsen-to-Leroy Kelly touchdown pass. But the Bengals hung tough, returning a fumble for a touchdown to secure a halftime lead, then secured a 20–16 advantage in the fourth quarter. The Browns gathered momentum in the final period, mounting a pair of touchdown drives to take a ten-point lead and, after a late Cincinnati score, hung on for a 30–27 victory that left everyone thirsty for more. "Two hundred and forty-four miles separate Cleveland from Cincinnati—fortunately," Edward Whelan wrote in the following morning's *Plain Dealer*. "If the two were any closer, there might be intrastate warfare."

As the final gun sounded, Collier jogged to midfield, presumably to shake Brown's hand. But, true to his word, Brown wasn't there. Cascaded by a chorus of boos from a capacity crowd that saw the move as unsportsmanlike, Brown trudged off the field, head down, looking like a deposed commander in chief. Which, in a way, he still was.

Taking a cue from the Bengals in their preseason meeting, the Browns presented Art Modell with a game ball afterward—which they likely wouldn't have done had the Browns defeated, say, the Kansas City Chiefs in the same fashion. Just another game, indeed.

Things got even worse for Brown's Bengals over the next few weeks, as their losing streak reached six games with a Monday-night loss in Pittsburgh. Trailing the first-place Browns by three games with seven to play, it appeared Cincinnati's first NFL season would be a disappointment.

After a blowout win in Buffalo ended the skid, the Bengals returned home for a rematch with the Browns. The second encounter would play out beneath an ominous cloud hovering over the sports world, with kickoff just hours after the Marshall University football team was killed in a tragic plane crash in Huntington, West Virginia. Before an overcapacity crowd of 60,007—the largest ever to witness a sporting event in Cincinnati—the Browns jumped to a quick 7–0 lead, just as they had in their first trip to Riverfront three months before. They were poised to make the advantage fourteen when they then drove inside the Cincinnati 10. But the Bengals defense stood strong, forcing Cleveland to settle for a field goal that made it 10–0. It seemed like a minor detail at the time but wound up being the turning point of the game.

The Browns offense, led by rookie quarterback Mike Phipps—making his first NFL start in place of the injured Bill Nelsen—was held scoreless for the remainder of the cold afternoon, and the Bengals clawed back into it. Amid random bursts of snow flurries, they surged ahead, 14–10, late in the third quarter and hung on for their third NFL victory. This time leaving the field triumphant, Brown sprinted toward the locker room, taking off his familiar hat and waving to the crowd in an emotional gesture he admitted to not remembering later. In the locker room afterward, he said he felt like he was eighteen years old again. When asked point-blank if this was his greatest victory, he admitted that it was. "This one," he told reporters, "makes it worth all the while." He'd even visibly wept when his players had given him the game ball. Clearly, we were done with the "just another game" charade.

The victory meant even more in retrospect, as it completely turned around the Bengals' season. Aided by a favorable schedule, they roared to seven consecutive wins—a streak that wouldn't be matched by another Bengals team for forty-five years—and caught the sputtering Browns in the standings on Thanksgiving weekend.

Following an ugly Cleveland loss to Dallas in Week Thirteen, the Bengals surged ahead in the standings and controlled their destiny going into the final week. All they needed was a victory at Riverfront over the 2–11 Boston Patriots, and the first-ever AFC Central title would be theirs. Behind three touchdowns by running back Paul Robinson, Cincinnati sprinted to a 38–0 halftime lead and coasted to a 45–7 victory. As the clock hit zero, Paul Brown's players hoisted him on their shoulders and carried him from the field, just beneath a large banner hung from the upper deck reading, "Thank You, Art Modell." It was the defining moment of what may have been Brown's most impressive season, which fittingly ended with him being named the NFL's Coach of the Year. "Personally, this is my little dream come true," Brown said after the game. "This has been the most interesting and gratifying season I've ever known."

And while the Bengals' 8–6 mark was only good enough to qualify for the playoffs because of the ramshackle quality of the AFC Central, under the circumstances, it was still something to behold. At the time, it was the fastest any expansion team had ever reached the postseason. The *Plain Dealer*'s Bob Dolgan labeled Brown's performance as one of the all-time greatest coaching jobs in the history of sports. "It's classic drama," Dolgan wrote, "with the exiled genius coming back to win a title in his old age with a bunch of boys." He even suggested that Hollywood should turn the story into a movie, with Gregory Peck playing Brown and Tony Curtis playing Art Modell.

Adding to the legend, Brown had accomplished it all without his starting quarterback and hope for the future. Greg Cook was everything the Bengals could have hoped for when they snagged him with the fifth overall pick in the 1969 draft. Born in Dayton and a star at the University of Cincinnati, he provided a local connection as well as bankable promise. Even when his career got off to a rough start after he injured his shoulder in his third game and he missed a month of action, he bounced back to put together an impressive season and was named the AFL's Rookie of the Year. It turned out to be both the sunrise and sunset of his career.

Cook injured the rotator cuff in his right shoulder in a pickup basketball game the following winter and not only missed the entire season, but never fully recovered. It would be three years before Cook would play again, and then just long enough to complete one pass before hanging it up and leading to one of the great "what-if" debates in Bengals history. Virgil Carter—picked up after being cut by Buffalo just two weeks before the season began—filled in admirably in 1970 and directed the Bengals to seven of their eight wins.

Cincinnati's upstart campaign ended with a lopsided loss to eventual Super Bowl-champion Baltimore in the divisional playoffs. But just as he'd done twenty years before, Paul Brown had surprised everyone by taking a team into the postseason in its first year in the NFL. Suddenly, it was the young and improving Bengals who appeared to be the team of the future, and the aging Browns who seemed to be facing years of rebuilding—symbolized by the retirement of Blanton Collier after the season.

Ironically, the first half of the 1971 season seemed to be a rinse-and-repeat of 1970. Not only did the Bengals stumble out of the starting gate again, but the Browns built a comfortable division lead with an exciting win over their new Ohio rivals. Trailing 24–13 in the fourth quarter at Riverfront in mid-October, the Browns scored a pair of late touchdowns—the last with thirty-nine seconds remaining—to hand Cincinnati a stunning loss and push their record to 4–1. Mirroring their start the year before, the Bengals dropped to 1–7 after a seven-game losing streak that saw them again lose their starting quarterback. Virgil Carter went down with a separated shoulder in Week Four and would miss the next month. Once again in desperation mode, Paul Brown turned to an unknown rookie that he eventually would rank just behind Otto Graham as the greatest quarterback in history. A skinny kid from Augustana College named Ken Anderson filled in admirably as he embarked upon what would be a fantastic career.

Once Carter returned, the Bengals rallied for three straight victories that pulled them back into the race in a once-again-mediocre AFC Central. With the script unfolding much as it had the year before, on the first weekend of December they traveled to Cleveland for a rematch with the struggling Browns—still limping from a four-game losing streak—with a chance to pull within a game of first place with two more to play. Though the unique nature of the relationship between the two teams was just over a year old at this point, it had already taken root. "It's like I would like to beat my own brother," Dick Schafrath confessed going into the contest.

For the fourth straight time, the Browns and Bengals put on a terrific show. The Browns surged ahead with a touchdown on the game's third play following a Cincinnati fumble on the opening kickoff, but the Bengals rebounded to take a 20–7 lead in the final minute of the second quarter. A forty-six-yard scoring pass from Bill Nelsen to the amazingly named Fair Hooker five seconds before the half brought the Browns back to life, and they surged ahead on the first possession of the third quarter. Then the Bengals' Essex Johnson broke free for an eighty-six-yard touchdown run on the first play of the fourth quarter to put Cincinnati up, 27–21. The Bengals were again on the brink of torpedoing Cleveland's season.

After the Browns narrowed the margin to three, a long field-goal attempt by Cincinnati sailed wide left with just under seven minutes to play. Behind the determined running of Leroy Kelly, the Browns slowly marched down the field and scored the winning points on a short Kelly touchdown run with 1:48 remaining. An interception a play later clinched the victory and the division title for the Browns, who went on to post a 9–5 mark and, like the Bengals the year before, get skunked by Baltimore in the playoffs. Cincinnati, meanwhile, wobbled to a 4–10 finish, and once again, the Browns and Bengals appeared to be sailing in opposite directions.

With the rivalry already full of flavor, some new spice was added in 1972. Picking up on the success of the teams' initial preseason tilt—and the trend of NFL exhibitions throughout the late 1960s and early 1970s to play practice games in new and occasionally bizarre markets—over the next three seasons, the Browns and Bengals played an annual exhibition game in Columbus.

Initially, it was the greatest thing to happen in Columbus since the state capital moved there from Chillicothe. The first exhibition, held on Labor Day weekend, drew a whopping 84,000 fans to rain-soaked Ohio Stadium, which would turn out to be the largest crowd to ever witness a Browns-Bengals game. It marked Paul Brown's first trip to Ohio Stadium since his days at Great Lakes Academy nearly thirty years earlier, and the entire day was steeped in Buckeye State flavor. Woody Hayes watched from the press box, the OSU marching band performed, and Cleveland native Bob Hope was honored as "Mr. Ohio" at halftime. All they were missing was a flyover by the Wright Brothers.

A year later, the exhibition drew better than 73,000, but by the third time around, the bloom was off the rose. Just over 36,000 showed up— barely a third of the stadium's capacity and the smallest crowd for a game there since World War II. Both sides realized that now that the initial novelty had worn off, three games between the teams each year was too many. Thus ended not only the Columbus game experiment, but Browns-Bengals preseason contests in general.

The Browns-Bengals duel atop the division became a three-way battle in 1972 with the sudden emergence of the Pittsburgh Steelers as a championship contender. The Bengals avoided the crippling starts of the previous two seasons and sprinted to a 4–1 record—with the only loss a 27–6 rout in Cleveland in what was the first blowout of the series. Still in contention the next-to-last-week, the Bengals hosted the Browns with revenge and playoff positioning on the line. In the only Saturday meeting between the two, Cleveland surged to a 14–0 lead. Cincinnati fought back to tie the game at twenty-four going into the fourth period, but the Browns pulled it out on a late Don Cockroft field goal and secured the AFC's lone wild-card spot in the playoffs. The Bengals— who'd now dropped five of their six games against the Browns and failed to make the postseason the last two years after winning the division in 1970—watched the Browns' playoff loss to the undefeated Miami Dolphins on television.

As was becoming their custom, the Browns and Bengals flipped roles the following year. They each hovered around the .500 mark for the first half of the season as defending division champ Pittsburgh built a commanding lead. Then the Bengals made their move. Mirroring their remarkable finish from three years earlier, Cincinnati won its final six games, including a seventeen-point thumping of the Browns at Riverfront.

Aided by a last-minute Browns upset of the Steelers Thanksgiving weekend, the Bengals caught Pittsburgh and finished the season tied with the Steelers at 10–4. Based on the third tiebreaker—a better record against AFC opponents (7–3 to Pittsburgh's 6–4)—the Bengals (with an assist from the Browns, who'd finished an unorthodox 7–5–2) had captured their second division title. Another playoff pounding followed, this time to the defending Super Bowl-champion Dolphins in the Orange Bowl. But the Bengals had turned a corner and, for the first time in their history, had become a genuine title contender.

Hopes were understandably high in '74, particularly after a 4–1 start that included a pair of washouts over the suddenly floundering Browns. Then an Old Testament-esque blight of injuries doomed the season. Eight Cincinnati starters went down, and the Bengals limped across the finish line with six losses in their final nine games.

The Browns, meanwhile, *collapsed* across the finish line. The gradual diminishing of skills—to borrow a phrase Art Modell would use two decades later—of the first years of the early '70s turned into complete freefall in 1974 as the Browns suffered through the worst season in their history. They lost five of their first six games—four by at least ten points—and staggered to a 4–10 record, just their second losing mark in the twenty-nine-year history of the franchise. And perhaps just as disturbing for Art Modell, that season marked the Bengals' first-ever season sweep of the Browns, capped by Paul Brown's first and, as it turned out, only win at Cleveland Stadium against his former team.

As the Browns began the long process of rebuilding, the Bengals pushed full speed ahead toward a championship. With his team back at full strength, Paul Brown directed his Bengals toward the finest season in their history in 1975. Starting with a victory over the Browns on opening day, they won their first six games and took over first place in the AFC Central. They remained there well into November, when they traveled to Cleveland for what appeared would be another unremarkable chapter in the series.

Never before and never since has a Browns-Bengals game represented the teams at such polar extremes. At 8–1, the Bengals held the best record in the AFC and were gunning for home-field advantage throughout the playoffs. The Browns, meanwhile, had hit rock bottom, losing their first nine games in 1975, six by at least two touchdowns. A gallows humor had developed around the once-proud franchise. Prior to the game, a stadium police officer motioned up to the fans who'd bothered to show up. "Watch it," he said to a colleague. "They may jump today."

Surprising everyone, likely even themselves, the woeful Browns put forth a spirited effort on a sunshiny November Sunday. Running back Billy LeFear returned the opening kickoff ninety-two yards to the Cincinnati two-yard line—and, reflecting the Browns' luck in 1975, suffered a career-ending broken leg on the tackle. A touchdown by budding young star Greg Pruitt on the next play put the Browns ahead, and a field goal later in the period made it 9–0. The small but spirited home crowd began to take notice. Things returned to normal over the next fifteen minutes as the Bengals exploded for twenty points to take command of the game and led, 23–12, early in the third quarter. After a Cleveland field goal cut the margin to eight midway through the period, Ken Anderson—who'd by now emerged as one of the NFL's top quarterbacks and thrown for a franchise-record 447 yards in a Monday-night victory over Buffalo six days earlier—took a hard hit from Browns defensive end Jerry Sherk and left the game with a bruised chest. The high-flying Cincinnati offense went into reverse, and the Browns crept closer. Playing the finest game of his career, embattled quarterback Mike Phipps directed a pair of fourth-quarter touchdown drives to push the Browns into the lead.

With the clock ticking down under three minutes, Cleveland defensive back Jim Hill intercepted a pass by Bengals backup quarterback John Reaves and returned it fifty-six yards for the game-clinching touchdown. It snapped the Browns' eleven-game losing streak and delivered one of their sweetest victories in years. The fans who'd started the afternoon on suicide watch stormed the field and swarmed the players they'd been booing all year. "Something about these Cincinnati Bengals," Chuck Heaton wrote in Monday's *Plain Dealer*, "brings out the best in the Browns."

The Bengals rebounded to finish with an 11–3 record and secure their third playoff berth in six years. But this trip to the playoffs ended just like the previous two. Trailing by seventeen in the fourth quarter against the Raiders in Oakland, the Bengals cut the margin to three with five minutes to play, then recovered a fumble in Oakland territory. But a Ted Hendricks sack of Ken Anderson thwarted the ensuing drive, and the Raiders hung on for a 31–28 win that, four days later, would prove to have much more historical significance.

***

It seems counterintuitive, but throughout his best season in Cincinnati with his best Bengals team yet, Paul Brown couldn't help but think about retiring. He was sixty-seven years old, and 1975 marked his forty-first season as a head coach. It's easy to look at the situation and wonder why, with the Bengals finally firmly planted among the NFL's elite, he didn't hang around for another year or two to see if he could land a Super Bowl before departing the sideline.

But in typical Paul Brown fashion, there was no drama or inner turmoil about it. He felt he had nothing more to prove and wanted to leave the game on a good note. He'd repeatedly rebuked accusations that the game had passed him by, even breezing past Houston coach Sid Gillman calling him "senile." And yet, even Brown admitted that he wasn't crazy about the direction the game was going. He hated dealing with agents—which many players were beginning to use—and despised the growing influence of the players union.

On New Year's Day 1976, he picked up the telephone and called the Bengals' PR director to tell him the news so he could deliver it to the media. Hours into America's bicentennial year, Paul Brown's coaching career was over.

It stunned not only the football world, but rocked the Bengals franchise as if a hurricane had swept in off the Ohio River. There'd been no mention of his stepping down at his final staff meeting two days before, and many assistant coaches learned of his decision when they watched the evening news. Brown himself was at his winter home in California, so there was no press conference or even any interviews so Brown could explain. Just like that, with one phone call, arguably the greatest coaching career in football history was over.

The Bengals would begin a new chapter, just as the Browns had the year before. And just as their narratives had overlapped with Paul Brown, so too would they with another coach over the better part of the next decade.

4

New Browns, New Bengals
1999–2002

It was, unquestionably, the lowest point in the thirty-year history of the rivalry. Like watching two drunk uncles argue at Thanksgiving, both wrong and neither wearing pants.

The Browns had returned to the NFL in 1999 as an expansion team, albeit a truly miserable one. The hastily-put-together roster consisted of a collection of cast-offs and rookies that were comically overmatched against even an average team. But, as had been the case throughout the 1990s, the Cincinnati Bengals were no average team, embodied by a pitiful stretch going into 1999 in which they lost fourteen of fifteen games. Established though they might have been, the Bengals represented the new Browns' best chance to capture their first win.

And here they were in Week Five: the 0–4 Browns hosting the 0–4 Bengals. The league's worst offense against the league's worst defense. The hopeless expansion team matching the chronically incompetent cellar dweller punchline for punchline. It was only mid-October, but it felt like the overall No. 1 draft pick was on the line.

Somewhere, Paul Brown was looking down at his former teams and wishing desperately to be looking at something else.

How had it come to this? How had the fierce Browns-Bengals contests of the early 1970s devolved into the cacophony of nonsense played out at brand-new Cleveland Browns Stadium on October 10, 1999? It was a game that was the "Yakety Sax" theme song away from a Benny Hill sketch. A game that, like the sun, hurt your eyes to look at.

But what made this game a true retrospective mess was the controversial subplot that surrounded the teams' two completely overwhelmed rookie quarterbacks.

Looking back now at the first few picks of the 1999 draft, literally everything that took place is laughable. The Browns, granted the top pick as an expansion team, felt they had an embarrassment of riches, a smorgasbord of football talent to choose from. But ultimately, they were torn between a pair of quarterbacks, either one of which, they decided, could be the centerpiece they could build their new franchise around.

Tim Couch or Akili Smith.

For all the hand-wringing and finger-pointing that would come later, in that fateful spring of 1999, the Browns truly felt they couldn't go wrong. Either player, they assumed, could blossom into a star. It's a concept that today is like trying to make sense of Y2K paranoia. But at the time, it was actually a thing.

Couch had been the favorite for months. Tall and athletic, he'd been something of a college legend. Kentucky born and bred, he was like an urban myth coming out of high school, setting all kinds of state records. With bluegrass essentially running through his veins, he stayed close to home and chose to play at the University of Kentucky, a program that always generated excitement among UK fans because the start of football season meant that it was almost the start of basketball season.

But Couch had put the football Wildcats on the map, leading them to heretofore unseen heights and helping transform UK's offense into one of the best in the nation during his sophomore season. As a junior, Couch threw for better than 4,200 yards and led the Wildcats to seven wins—their best tally in fourteen years—and a spot in the Outback Bowl, where he threw for 336 yards in a loss to Penn State. A Heisman Trophy finalist and the SEC's Player of the Year, Couch had demonstrated an ability to single-handedly throw a subpar program over his shoulder like a sack of potatoes and carry it into a steakhouse-themed bowl game. This was understandably appealing to the Browns' brass, who already anticipated just how dreadful expansion football would be.

But coming up along the rail hard and fast as draft day approached was Akili Smith, who even just six months before wasn't being considered a first-round pick, let alone going No. 1 overall. Two years older than Couch, Smith had already been there and back with his athletic career, giving pro baseball a shot out of high school and spending three unremarkable seasons in the minors. Smith then decided to try football, and after a pit stop in junior college, he transferred to the University of Oregon. Named the starter for his senior year, Smith lit up the PAC-10 in his eleven starts, throwing for 3,700 yards and thirty-two touchdowns in leading the Ducks to an 8–4 record and a bowl bid.

To be fair, you can see why both Couch and Smith generated attention. But looking back, the problems that would ultimately lead to a lot of long Sundays were apparent. For Couch, that he played in a gimmicky, throw-spaghetti-at-the-wall-and-see-what-sticks offense. In fact, in the weeks leading up to the draft, the Browns discovered that Couch had spent his career gripping the football the wrong way and, more troubling, that Kentucky's offense didn't actually use a playbook. For Smith, the issue was sample size—lots of guys put together one great college season, but was he good enough to do the same kind of thing at the professional level? Warning signs aside, many NFL teams were ensorcelled with both. None more than the two teams from Ohio.

The Bengals loved Akili Smith and really wanted him with the third pick. They'd even turned down a trade offer of eight or nine different draft picks from delirious New Orleans coach Mike Ditka, who wanted University of Texas running back Ricky Williams so badly he staked his entire career on it. Mike Brown admitted it was a comically generous offer that the Bengals could have milked for years to come, but they felt that now was the time to get a quarterback.

The Bengals hated the idea of the Browns taking Smith before they could and couldn't stand having to wait to see what their northern neighbors would do. And whether intentionally or not, the Browns made the Bengals squirm. Couch and Smith appeared side by side on the cover of *Sports Illustrated* the week before the draft, alongside Browns super-fan Big Dawg John Thompson, with the message clear: the Browns had their pick of the litter and just couldn't decide.

Even when they'd determined that Smith had surpassed Couch, they still leaned toward the Kentucky star, giving him another chance to shine at a personal workout the week before the draft. When he redeemed himself and surged back ahead of Smith, the Browns settled on Couch and began negotiating, wanting to have a contract in place before his name was announced. The Browns and Couch's agent dickered through the night before the draft, with Akili Smith still hovering in the background. If a deal couldn't be brokered with Couch, the Browns were willing to go back to Smith. Both quarterbacks spent that sleepless Friday night wondering if they might be the No. 1 overall pick the next day.

Just after dawn, the Browns and Couch agreed to a deal, and a few hours later, he was on stage wearing a Browns cap and holding up a Browns jersey. After the Philadelphia Eagles grabbed quarterback Donovan McNabb from Syracuse, the Bengals selected Smith, who, in a response that was strange in its repetition and intensity, was more irritated with the Browns than happy with the Bengals. "I was leverage all the way," he bemoaned, later, claiming that the Browns had "left him at the altar" after never having any true intention of drafting him. Endearing himself to his new team and fan base, he vowed revenge against the Browns and said he did see an instant connection between himself and Paul Brown—both had been rejected by Cleveland.

Couch began minicamp practice with the expansion Browns a week later, and following weeks of predraft speculation and drama, Smith became a Bengal—after holding out for twenty-seven days and missing most of training camp, that is.

Everyone expected that the Couch-Smith incident would rekindle the Browns-Bengals rivalry, which had lost some of its spice with Paul Brown and Art Modell both now out of the picture. "We're going to be competing for the rest of our lives," Smith predicted. Mike Brown also saw a bright future for both, suggesting that they'd play against one another thirty times.

Or, as it turned out, twice.

***

The general rule of thumb with rookie quarterbacks is to not play them right away. Tempting as it is to crack open all that promising talent, most agree it takes at least a year for a first-year signal caller to acclimate to the NFL and his new team's offensive system. That becomes increasingly more difficult when the rookie is made a starter right away. Both the Browns and Bengals ignored this common-sense warning. Couch and Smith both saw action in Week One, and Couch was named the full-time starter the following week. Though Smith got considerable playing time in two of the next three games, the Bengals managed to wait until Week Five to anoint Smith their new starting quarterback. He would make his first start—where else—in Cleveland against the Browns, and Smith would get his shot at revenge right off the rip.

With intrigue swirling around the battle of winless teams like flies at a landfill, the contest actually turned out to be entertaining. The Bengals dominated total yardage and time of possession, but the Browns were in control much of the game. Smith directed a pair of long drives to begin his first start, but both stalled inside the Cleveland 10 and ended with field goals. The Browns took advantage and surged ahead on a clever fake field goal that saw kicker Phil Dawson scamper into the end zone for the team's first rushing touchdown of the season. A Cincinnati fumble on the ensuing kickoff, aided by a long pass interference penalty a play later, set up a second score, and the Browns surged ahead 14–6— which would turn out to be the largest lead they would hold in their first fifteen games.

Smith's first career touchdown pass just before the half capped another long drive and cut the margin to two, where it remained through the third quarter. A blocked Bengals punt led to a Cleveland field goal in the first minute of the fourth and a 17–12 Cleveland lead. The Browns' first victory was within reach, particularly after Smith was stuffed for no gain on fourth-and-one from the Cincinnati 44 with 3:50 remaining. But having neither the experience nor the talent to land the knockout punch, the Browns were unable to run out the clock, and Smith and the Bengals regained possession at their own 20 with two minutes to play.

Thus began the first and last memorable moment of Akili Smith's career. He completed four straight passes to drive the Bengals into Cleveland territory, the last of which converted a do-or-die fourth-and-four at the Cleveland 29 with thirty-two seconds left. Smith's next pass fell incomplete, but the Browns were penalized for pass interference, giving Cincinnati a first down at the Cleveland 2. After two incompletions, Smith lobbed an arching pass into the end zone that Carl Pickens reeled in for the winning touchdown with nine seconds remaining. Smith pounded his chest, cupped his hand to his ear, and ran his finger across his neck in a slit-throat gesture toward the stands and the Browns bench in an extended disco version of taunting the home crowd and the Cleveland franchise in general.

Afterward, Smith compared the game to the Super Bowl, and columnists in both cities declared the rivalry revived and potentially as good as ever. In reality, the Browns had simply remained winless and the Bengals had merely managed to avoid the embarrassment of losing to an expansion team—though just barely.

Still, it looked like Smith could turn out to be an NFL player after all, throwing for 221 yards and a pair of scores while leading his team from behind with a clutch, last-minute touchdown drive. He said he'd played as if it were the last game of his life. And, as it turned out, he was basically right, since his personal Vengeance Bowl essentially marked the beginning and end of his NFL career. Three weeks later, a sprained right toe ended his season, and things would only get worse the following year.

Couch, meanwhile, hung in there. Taking repeated beatings behind a scattershot offensive line, he delivered the new Browns' first victory in New Orleans on Halloween with a fifty-six-yard Hail Mary pass on the game's final play. Two weeks later, a last-second field goal at Three Rivers Stadium delivered a one-point Browns win over a Steelers team that had throttled Cleveland by forty-three points on opening night. But the expansion miseries soon returned, and the Browns closed the season with six straight losses, including a let's-just-get-through-this blowout at the hands of the Bengals in Week Fourteen in the final NFL game ever played at Riverfront Stadium.

The 44–28 win over the Browns marked the Bengals' third straight after a 1–10 start—once again providing false hope at the end of a miserable campaign. They finished 4–12, barely topping the Browns' 2–14 mark. Neither team had much reason for excitement going into the new millennium, but both were confident their respective young quarterbacks would carry their franchises over the hump.

As if purposely extending the soap opera drama, the teams would meet right away in 2000. After the NFL's puzzling decision to give the Bengals their bye week in Week One (right up there with giving the Browns the final week of the season off each of their first two years back), Ohio's NFL teams would square off in Week Two, when they would break a bottle of champagne over Paul Brown Stadium's proverbial bow.

Quarterback drama aside, who better to provide the opposition for the first game in the new ballpark than the other team Paul Brown was associated with? Mike Brown's $450 million, taxpayer-funded rumpus room was packed to the brim on an overcast September Sunday, with most fans simply assuming they'd be watching a continuation of what the Bengals had done to the Browns in their last meeting nine months before. But the sophomore version of the new Browns turned out to be quite a different animal, or at least started the season that way.

On Paul Brown Stadium's very first play, Tim Couch completed a sixty-five-yard pass to wideout David Patten to the Cincinnati 11. In typical Browns fashion, they managed not to score, but the tone was set. Soon after, the Browns broke a 7–7 tie with a short Couch touchdown pass early in the second quarter. It gave them a lead they wouldn't relinquish but also cost them a starting offensive lineman when Jim Pyne blew out his knee leaping up to celebrate with his teammates in the end zone.

They extended the lead to ten and then seventeen points in the second half, and the Bengals never threatened to make a game of it. The capacity crowd, eager to test out the new stadium's escalators and turnstiles, filed out well before the final gun just as they'd done countless times at Riverfront over the previous decade. Not only was getting slobberknockered in your inaugural game in a half-billion-dollar stadium by a rival that had won only twice the year before bad enough, but the Bengals' franchise quarterback looked worse than ever. Matched against the same defense he'd shredded on the game-winning drive a year earlier, Smith completed only fifteen of forty-three passes, was intercepted twice, and was sacked seven times. Tim Couch, meanwhile, looked poised and in command in leading his team to victory. For the first time, it looked like the Browns had made a good decision in the 1999 draft, particularly when compared to the road not taken.

And so it would go for Akili Smith over the next few months. He started the next ten games with equally troubling results: six interceptions to only three touchdowns, a miserable 44 percent completion rate, sacked thirty-six times, and a mind-numbing passer rating of 52.8. With Cincinnati at 2–9, new head coach Dick LeBeau—who'd replaced beleaguered Bruce Coslet three games into the season—benched Smith in favor of journeyman Scott Mitchell, who really wasn't much better as the Bengals staggered to a second straight 4–12 record.

In Porky Pig fashion, that was basically all, folks, for Akili Smith. With free agent Jon Kitna arriving from Seattle to assume the starting quarterback role in 2001, Smith was Masterlocked to the bench and didn't even appear in a game until Week Eleven, when he was thrown out there for some quality garbage time during a Bengals shutout loss—naturally—in Cleveland. Begging to be traded, he would start just two more games over the next two seasons and was finally, mercifully, released in 2003.

He never was able to catch on with another team, even after attempts in NFL Europe and the Canadian Football League. He would eventually go down as one of the biggest draft busts in NFL history. The No. 3 pick in the 1999 draft completed less than 47 percent of his pass attempts and threw only five touchdown passes in his NFL career. Altogether, he played in a grand total of twenty-two games, starting seventeen.

He won three of them—two over the Cleveland Browns.

***

When you compare Tim Couch to Akili Smith, he really wasn't that bad of a draft pick.

But only when you make that comparison.

Almost exactly one year after the Bengals released Smith, the Browns released Couch. Statistically speaking, the Browns got more return on their investment than the Bengals did from Smith. But in some ways, Couch's journey from draft day to release day was much more agonizing and certainly more drawn out.

After a promising start to the 2000 season that saw the Browns win two of their first three games with Couch apparently developing nicely, disaster struck—as it usually did with the Browns in the post-Paul Brown reality. In a mid-October practice, Couch's throwing hand struck an onrushing teammate, and the quarterback's right thumb broke. Just like that, he was done for the year. With backup/designated mentor Ty Detmer already lost for the season to a preseason injury, the Browns turned to Doug Pedersen, wheelbarrowed in off the scrap heap, and sixth-round draft choice Spergon Wynn to lead the ship to shore.

Needless to say, with the already-wobbly Browns forced to go to Options C and D at quarterback along with a myriad of other injuries, things got ugly. *Real* ugly. They lost eight of their last nine, five by at least twenty-one points, as they reached levels of abomination the '99 expansion team only had sweaty nightmares about. Along the way was a 12–3 home loss to Cincinnati, in which Akili Smith picked up his final win as a starting quarterback (despite a dismal passer rating of 27.9 for the day), while Pedersen and Wynn took turns drawing the short straw to run the moribund Browns offense. None of the three quarterbacks completed 50 percent of his passes, and neither offense topped 260 total yards. It was, then and now, a strong candidate for the worst NFL game ever played.

When the torment was finally over, the Browns finished 3–13—technically a game better than 1999, but with far more psychological damage done. Head Coach Chris Palmer—who was only hired because their initial choice, Brian Billick, was hesitant to commit and was eventually snapped up by Art Modell in Baltimore—was made the scapegoat after the season and promptly fired. Butch Davis was trotted in to resuscitate the Browns, just as he'd done in turning around the perpetually scandal-crippled University of Miami program.

As the Browns hit the reset button in record time, Cleveland fans watched the only two remaining nightmare scenarios unfold. Behind the leadership of the head coach whom they'd wanted to hire and general manager Ozzie Newsome, who'd spent his career as a Hall of Fame tight end with the Browns, the Baltimore Ravens cruised to a blowout victory in Super Bowl XXXV. Art Modell finally had his Lombardi Trophy, and the Cuyahoga River nearly bubbled with the heat of the rage in Northeast Ohio. A year later, it happened again when Bill Belichick won his first Super Bowl in his second year with the New England Patriots.

Despite the constant reaffirmations that the universe truly hated them, the Browns endured. With Davis bringing a new energy and the roster staying relatively healthy, Couch turned in a promising season in 2001. They roared to a 3–1 start and stood at 6–4 and right in the thick of the playoff chase after a shutout victory over the Bengals Thanksgiving weekend. Reality caught up with the still-in-over-their-heads Browns, and they lost five of their last six.

But it was the third of those losses that everyone would remember— a game defined by one of the most ridiculous and frightening incidents in NFL history.

The type of thing that would only seem to happen to a team that was genuinely haunted.

***

By December 2001, instant replay had been a part of the NFL for nearly fifteen years. Not the slow-motion regurgitation of the previous play shown on television—that had been a part of the game since the mid-16th century. But rather the ability for the officials to review a play via video monitor and then change the initial ruling on the field if there was evidence to support it.

The Browns had something of a history with instant replay. They were involved with its first-ever instance just minutes into its initiation in 1986 to determine whether a fumble recovered by safety Al Gross at Chicago's Soldier Field was a touchdown or a safety. Two years later, a pair of controversial instant replay rulings cost the Browns a playoff game.

In general, instant replay caused as many problems as it solved, and it was discontinued in 1991. But it continued to be discussed among league officials and owners, and eventually the system and technology were enhanced and reintroduced in 1999—just in time for the Browns' return to the NFL. They managed to avoid any tragic run-ins with the newfangled system for two full years. But when they finally did, they got their money's worth.

The 2001 Browns were still weeble-wobbling along in the playoff race, taking a 6–6 record into a Week Fourteen encounter with Jacksonville at Cleveland Browns Stadium. For much of the game, the Browns underachieved, and they trailed throughout. But down just 15–10 with three minutes remaining, they took possession at their own thirty-four with one last chance to pull out a victory. With Couch at the helm, they meandered into Jacksonville territory and faced fourth-and-two from the twelve with 1:08 left. Couch tossed a short pass to wide receiver Quincy Morgan, who caught it at the nine for an apparent first down. But Morgan appeared to lose his grip on the football as he hit the ground. With the clock ticking down under a minute, the Browns rushed to the line of scrimmage, quickly snapped the ball, and Couch spiked it into the ground to stop the clock.

As he did, first-year referee Terry McAulay received an electronic signal on the buzzer hooked to his belt. Under the revised instant replay rules, within the last two minutes of a half or a game, a designated replay official watching on a monitor high above the field would closely examine any play that included a borderline aspect. The replay official would quickly determine whether that play deserved further review and send an electronic signal to the field officials, who would then trot over to an on-field monitor along the sideline and take a look.

But one of the cardinal rules of instant replay—in both of its iterations—was that once the next play had been run, the play in question could not be reviewed. Morgan's would-be catch qualified as borderline and deserved to be looked at, but the signal requesting a review came after Couch had spiked the ball on the following play. Thus, according to fifteen years of instant replay etiquette, that ship had sailed. Just or not, by rule, the game should have continued, as it had countless times in similar situations before.

Not so fast, claimed McAulay. Citing a malfunction in the communication system, he stated that the signal had actually been sent before the snap of the next play. Therefore, they could indeed go back and review Morgan's catch. There were instantly a couple problems with that explanation—one, the rule had never been about when the signal was sent or received, but when the officials on the field stopped the action. No whistle had been blown prior to or during the ensuing play, which was the only measure that counted. More important, however, replays of the incident showed McAulay not glancing down at the buzzer on his belt until *after* Couch's spike.

McAulay went over to the peep-show tent on the Browns sideline that contained the replay monitor, rewound the tape to Morgan's catch, and, predictably, ruled that it wasn't, in fact, a catch. Therefore, the Browns had failed to convert on fourth down, and Jacksonville would now regain possession with forty-eight seconds remaining, essentially ending the ball game.

"Berzerk" is a word not often used in sports, primarily because it rarely is an apt description of what transpires within the confines of an athletic event. Considering what happened next, "berzerk" is on the money as a modifier. Debris—mostly half-filled plastic beer bottles flung from unhappy patrons, along with some radios and, ironically, a Tim Couch bobblehead—rained down onto the field and littered the end zones and sidelines. Players from both teams migrated away from the stands and gathered near midfield to stay clear of the fallout. Players were instructed to put their helmets on, and Jacksonville wide receiver Jimmy Smith said he felt like he was in *Saving Private Ryan*. Those unlucky enough not to be equipped with protective gear felt bottles bounce off their bodies. A security guard was clobbered in the forehead with a bottle thrown from the upper deck. The four-year-old child of another staff member was hit in the head with a cup. Several people were hit so hard, they bled.

After a few minutes of confusion and a handful of poor souls milling around on the wrong end of target practice, McAulay simply called the game. As the officials attempted to leave the field, they were pummeled by even more bottles, sending them ducking and sprinting into the tunnel beneath the stands.

Making things even more surreal, within minutes, NFL Commissioner Paul Tagliabue contacted the stadium and informed the officials they'd just made their second big mistake in five minutes—they didn't have the authority to end the game. There were still forty-eight seconds to play, and the league required both teams to drag themselves back out onto the field to see it through. At this point, nearly twenty minutes had passed since the final play, and many players had already removed their jerseys and equipment. With a mishmash of players spread across the field in various states of undress, the Jaguars took two snaps, knelt out the clock, and then got to reenact the dangerous leaving-the-field process once again.

The only thing more ridiculous than what happened on the field was the aftermath. In an odd move, Browns president Carmen Policy refused to condemn the actions of the fans hurling the bottles that drew blood and terrified children:

> I am not criticizing the fans at all, because I don't think it's appropriate today. I think a lot has happened. The fans' hearts have been ripped out. I am not condoning what the fans did, and I'm not criticizing it. I am not condoning what the officials did.
>
> If I'm not going to criticize the officials, I'm certainly not going to criticize the fans of Cleveland. . . . If we won this way down in Jacksonville, I would expect it [the fan reaction]. We wouldn't criticize their fans, either.

Policy then took his nonchalant stance to the next level. "Those are plastic bottles and I don't think they carry much of a wallop," he said. "As a practical matter, we've seen situations in prior years at Cleveland Stadium, such as batteries being thrown. I don't think this is an example of life and limb being at risk. No one got hurt."

If he'd replaced the word "hurt" with "killed," he might have sounded less ridiculous. But clearly the fear of sounding ridiculous wasn't even on his radar. "I don't think Cleveland will take a black eye from this," he concluded. "I like the fact that our fans cared." Cared enough to drunkenly throw things at complete strangers—a characteristic we all respect.

It was a callous, unprofessional thing to say. Then Al Lerner, the Browns owner, backed him up. "It wasn't pleasant—I wouldn't suggest anything like that—but it wasn't World War III," he said. "People reacted and nobody for one second is condoning that, nor do we think they should plug in the electric chair as soon as they find each of those people."

The Browns got screwed out of a chance to win the game. But between the fans' mob mentality and Policy and Lerner's mob lawyer improv, that was no longer the point. The aftermath of the bad call represented everything that was wrong with football fans, painting them as dark and violent as British soccer hooligans.

Still, many fans—and really even the Browns owner and president—felt that their actions were justified. It led to a mini-investigation after the game to figure out exactly what had happened and why everything had gone wrong. When *Plain Dealer* reporter Tony Grossi asked about Couch's spike, McAulay matter-of-factly replied, "It never happened."

Ironically, there were many passes during Couch's career that people wish had never happened. In retrospect, it's refreshing to think that field officials had the power to wipe them from existence.

With the blown call, the terrifying aftermath, the self-serving response of the Browns brass, and the halfhearted cover-up by the officiating crew and the NFL, the incident would eventually earn the label "BottleGate."

When it was all over, the Browns' fledging playoff hopes were incinerated, and the fan base indeed suffered another black eye following another "only in Cleveland" moment. The national media rightfully spanked Browns fans for their inhuman behavior, and the incident instantly became one of the most appalling in the history of sports—right up there with the ten-cent beer night riot that resulted in a Cleveland Indians forfeit on the same hallowed, puke-stained ground twenty-seven years earlier.

It could have happened anywhere. With the tentative structure of instant replay in the final, frenzied minutes of a game, something like this was bound to happen somewhere. But it happened in Cleveland. And it's hard to see that as coincidental.

It was a head-on collision of three things Paul Brown abhorred about the game: lack of fundamentals (Morgan's inability to hang onto the pass), technological meddling (instant replay and its not-quite-fine-tuned apparatus), and a guerrilla fan base (operating almost exclusively on what the Native Americans referred to as "firewater"). Thus, in one fell swoop, it seemed that Paul Brown's ghost pulled a triple play:

cold-cocking the Browns, their fans, and NFL technology with one firm, backhanded slap.

Had this same incident played out elsewhere in front of less— "passionate" or "emotionally unstable," you make the call—fans, things wouldn't have gotten so ugly. During the confused madness, Jacksonville quarterback Mark Brunell, standing around with a pair of Browns defenders, commented, "I wish our fans cared this much." Only in the NFL would a comment like that make sense.

Somehow, the aftereffects didn't spill over onto McAulay. Three years later, he was anointed as head referee for the Super Bowl, an honor he'd receive twice more in the next decade. To Cleveland fans, this seemed like rewarding Gilligan for keeping everybody on the island. But to be fair, in the years between, McAulay did build a sterling reputation and was rated among the best officials in the league.

"Absolutely it was something no one should ever have to go through," he told the *Louisiana Times-Picayune* in 2009, "but I wouldn't be the guy I am today if I didn't learn from it. . . . So Cleveland, obviously I wish it hadn't happened, but I'm not sure I'd take it back. Because if it hadn't happened, would I have just worked my second Super Bowl? Maybe not."

Not unlike Bill Belichick, McAulay had used Cleveland as a training ground to work out his mistakes at the Browns' expense. Then moved on to bigger and better things, like winning the Super Bowl, which Belichick would do for the first time six weeks after BottleGate.

A bizarre, almost supernatural chain of events and poor judgment had cost the Browns a victory and defined an entire season. It was a perfect storm of conditions, a Halley's Comet-type of incident that you'd think would only happen once in a generation.

Three games later, it happened to the Browns again.

***

The opening game of Cleveland's 2002 season carried with it the expectations fans had for the fourth edition of Browns 2.0. After the Browns gradually increased their win total in their three seasons since returning to the NFL, everything pointed to a breakthrough year. Couch now had more than thirty-five starts under his belt, and the offense had collected a respectable number of weapons for him to work with. After a 7–9 finish in 2001, the expansion Browns' first winning record—and corresponding first playoff appearance—was anticipated and expected in 2002.

Week One seemed to back up that optimism. Even with Couch sidelined with a forearm injury, the Browns looked better than ever. Career backup Kelly Holcomb stepped in and directed a spectacular offensive performance that saw the Browns pile up more than 400 yards. But the Kansas City Chiefs matched them nearly yard for yard and point for point, and the teams rolled up and down Cleveland Browns Stadium. The Chiefs wiped out a thirteen-point fourth-quarter deficit, and the lead would change hands four times in the final eight minutes. After the Chiefs surged ahead, 37–36, with three minutes remaining, Holcomb drove the Browns right back down the field, and a Phil Dawson field goal gave them what appeared would be the game-winning points with twenty-nine seconds to play.

Out of time-outs, the Chiefs scurried near midfield with four seconds left. With time for just one more play, quarterback Trent Green dropped back to pass, was flushed out of the pocket, and was wrapped up by Cleveland linebacker Dwayne Rudd at the Kansas City 43. As Rudd was bringing him down, Green flipped a lateral to lineman John Tait, who began rumbling downfield as the Cleveland defense gradually pinned him along the sideline and eventually ran him out of bounds at the Cleveland 25. Game over, Browns win their opener for the first time in eight years. Right?

Nope.

In one of the most colossally stupid things ever to happen on a football field, Rudd, thinking he'd sacked Green and the play and game had ended then and there, bounced to his feet, ripped off his helmet, and threw it downfield in celebration. But just as had been the case the previous December, the officiating crew dug deep into the bowels of the rulebook and dusted off an obscure chestnut: any player taking his helmet off during a play shall be penalized for unsportsmanlike conduct. Had Green not lateraled the football and indeed had been sacked, Rudd's helmet removal would have been legal (though still bizarre) and the play would have been over. Thereby, Rudd foolishly removing his helmet would have been a case of no harm, no foul. But since Green did lateral the football, the play—lame duck as it was—was still alive, and Rudd's doffing of his cap constituted a fifteen-yard penalty. And it still might have been a salvageable situation had beefy John Tait not been permitted to lumber twenty-five yards downfield by the spread-out laissez-faire Cleveland defense. But he did, and since a game cannot end on a defensive penalty—a rote detail that, just like no play being reviewable after the next one is run, every fan knows—Rudd's unsportsmanlike conduct foul was assessed from the end of the play. Half the distance to the goal, first-and-ten from the Cleveland 12 for one untimed down.

Out trotted perhaps the most reliable kicker in NFL history, Morten Anderson, who calmly booted a thirty-yard chip shot through the uprights and into the heart of every Browns fan like an ice pick.

Once again, the Browns had managed to snatch defeat from the jaws of victory in never-before-seen fashion. And this time, there could be no complaining about technical difficulties or judgment calls. Obscure as the penalty may have been, there was no doubt about it. (Though there's an argument to be made that had Rudd not torn his helmet off literally inches in front of referee Ron Blum, he very likely would have gotten away with it.) The good news was that there was no fusillade of garbage launched by a furious fan base. The bitter home fans knew they'd been robbed of a victory once again, but this time it had been an inside job. "There may be no worse way to lose a football game," Tony Grossi wrote in the *Plain Dealer.* "Then again, stay tuned. The Browns are making macabre losses their unfortunate trademark."

It's difficult to imagine any team either coached or associated in any way with Paul Brown losing a game in such a fashion. Or if so, difficult to imagine the player responsible not being beaten to death with a two-by-four in the locker room afterward. Thus, once again, it was as if the Browns were being haunted by their namesake, who smote down a well-deserved victory because an undisciplined player had forgotten the fundamentals and wanted to show off.

It set the tone for a bizarre season—and yet still the most satisfying since the Browns returned to the NFL. The Dwayne Rudd debacle was the first of twelve Browns games in 2002 that were decided in the final minute of play, with breathtaking victories and soul-crushing defeats almost evenly split. A rally from a fourteen-point fourth-quarter deficit one week was countered by another unheard-of rule enforcement the next that saw the Browns block an overtime field-goal attempt in Pittsburgh, only to see the Steelers recover the loose ball and get to kick again. They rallied from a 21–3 hole to beat the playoff-bound Jets, then somehow lost at home to a miserable Carolina team that had dropped eight straight. They avenged BottleGate by beating Jacksonville on a Hail Mary caught (or, some would argue, not) by Quincy Morgan, then pissed away a sixteen-point second-half lead to lose a huge home game against Indianapolis. Over the course of this bungee-cord campaign is when most fans truly began to sour on Couch, whose inconsistencies and rookie mistakes were no longer forgivable now that he was in his fourth season.

With their bipolar campaign on the line, the Browns pulled out the biggest two games of the year. A last-minute touchdown secured a one-point win in Baltimore, and a critical goal-line stand in the final seconds clinched a win over Atlanta in the finale. With a few other games going their way that final weekend, the Browns clinched their first—and to date, still only—playoff berth of their new era.

And of course, a season like that needed a signature denouement. It came in Pittsburgh, where the underdog Browns stunned and dominated the Steelers for more than three-and-a-half quarters. With Kelly Holcomb getting the start in place of Couch, who'd broken his leg in the finale, the Browns' air attack was as brilliant as it had been in the opener four months earlier. Holcomb threw for 429 yards and three scores as the Browns dominated the game: up 14–0 early in the second quarter, 24–7 late in the third, and 33–21 midway through the fourth. But in true Browns fashion, they couldn't finish it off. Pittsburgh carved through a wheezing Cleveland defense for two long touchdown drives in the final six minutes, and that was it.

The Browns' schizophrenic bender into the postseason was over. And there were no more playoff trips coming.

***

Is it better to have loved and lost than never to have loved at all? Or, if Alfred Tennyson had been a football fan, is it better to have been through an excruciatingly emotional season defined by a painful playoff defeat than to have finished 2–14?

Any Cincinnati Bengals fan who endured the 2002 season would have unequivocally preferred the former.

While the Browns dragged their fans through four months of manic mood swings, the Bengals made their fans question their purpose in this world. After a somewhat promising 6–10 mark in 2001 that included three wins over playoff teams along with two straight victories to close out the season (there's that patent-pending Bengal tease again), they got off to a typical Cincinnati start the following year. They dropped their first seven games, this time failing to score more than seven points in five of their first six. A blowout win over the expansion Houston Texans and a squeaker over a New Orleans team that had already mailed it in by Week Sixteen were all the Bengals had to show for their efforts. It was not only the worst season in this sad string of bad seasons since Paul Brown's death, but the worst in franchise history, besting the quartet of 3–13 campaigns that had defined the 1990s.

With the Neil O'Donnell era now mercifully over, veteran cast-off Gus Frerotte was dragged in and forcibly thrust into the lineup at starting quarterback. After three miserable starts—symbolized by an ill-advised attempt by the right-handed Frerotte to throw a left-handed pass in Cleveland in Week Two that turned into a seventy-one-yard interception return—Frerotte was replaced. Not by Akili Smith, who just three years before was anointed the team's savior, but by fellow free agent afterthought Jon Kitna.

When it was mercifully over, the Bengals prepared to start all over again . . . again. Dick LeBeau stepped down as head coach, and they entered the draft looking for another franchise quarterback. Worse still, longtime standard-bearer Corey Dillon wanted out of Cincinnati after six straight thousand-yard seasons, just like star receiver Carl Pickens two years before. Eventually released a year after signing a five-year contract, Pickens had tried to accelerate his departure with vehement criticisms of Mike Brown and the Bengals front office, leading to the creation of a so-called "Pickens Clause" in all Cincinnati contracts going forward.

In essence, it was a loyalty oath every Bengals player had to agree to, forcing them to promise not to criticize Brown, team management, or the coaching staff. And if a player did so, he would forfeit his signing bonus money.

Perversely, the Pickens Clause prompted even more criticism, as once again, the Bengals were doing some groundbreaking in reverse, becoming the only NFL team to deliberately make itself look like a Gulag camp. Players, agents, and the NFL Players Association all hated the idea, and it served as a roadblock in contract negotiations that would lead to holdouts and ultimately deter players from wanting to come to Cincinnati at all.

Not that there was much reason to in the first place. The Bengals had now posted twelve straight nonwinning seasons, averaging more than eleven losses per year since Paul Brown had died. The growth of the Internet prompted a handful of new websites launched by ripshit fans dedicated not to following the Bengals, but berating them—highlighted by the infamous (and still operating) MikeBrownSucks.com. Their glistening new ballpark was both bankrupting the city and defined by empty seats and early departures each Sunday. And the stage for all this was a torn-up, moth-eaten field that suggested the Bengals were playing in your cousin's backyard.

From the leadership atop the franchise down to literally the ground they walked on, it appeared the Browns were on the rise and the Bengals were headed nowhere.

That would quickly change.

5

The Forrest Bump
1976-1983

The Bengals were on the rise, and the Browns were going nowhere. And it seemed as though the remainder of the 1970s would see the teams going in those same directions.

At the decade's midpoint, both franchises were settling into new chapters in their history as both brought in new coaches. The Bengals needed a replacement for Paul Brown following his abrupt retirement after the 1975 season, just as the Browns had the year before when veteran coach Nick Skorich stepped down after four generally mediocre seasons. Both teams wound up promoting from within, each elevating an offensive line coach who had no head coaching experience at any level. And one of the two would have a huge impact . . . on not just one of the teams, but both.

There's a trope of classic TV sitcoms about brothers dating the same girl. Either they both want to date her at the same time, or she breaks up with one to be with the other. In this story—just as throughout their histories—the Browns and Bengals were the brothers. And the girl they both dated was Forrest Gregg.

While many modern fans might not be familiar with Gregg, when he got into coaching, his unique name and chiseled face represented a golden age of professional football. A star tackle at Southern Methodist University, Gregg was drafted by the Green Bay Packers in 1956 and switched to guard, where he would be named All-Pro eight consecutive seasons. And it was no coincidence that just as Gregg entered his prime, the Packers became one of the great dynasties in football history, winning five NFL titles in seven years, including the first two Super Bowls. Vince Lombardi called Gregg the greatest player he ever coached. Which, translating that into a biblical analogy, was sort of like Jesus Christ naming his favorite apostle. And the apostle then riding the comment into a coaching career.

Naturally, as Gregg's long run as a player wound down, he was interested in transitioning into coaching. After Phil Bengsten took on the no-win job of replacing Lombardi as Green Bay's coach, Gregg was named as an unofficial player/coach in his final two seasons with the Packers (a concept that's downright hysterical today). When he was released by Green Bay after fourteen seasons in 1971, he signed with Dallas as an assistant but was forced back into uniform when injuries plagued the Cowboys' offensive line.

When he finally hung up the helmet for good, he joined the staff of the San Diego Chargers as offensive line coach. Then, after the 1973 season, he got a call from Art Modell. Gregg flew to Cleveland and was offered the same position with the Browns under Nick Skorich, who'd been Gregg's offensive line coach with Green Bay sixteen years before.

The Browns were dreadful in Gregg's first year in Cleveland, posting a franchise-worst 4–10 mark, and Skorich took the hint and retired after the season. As Modell began the search for a new head coach, he was drawn to the possibility of hiring Gregg, even despite his relative inexperience. After a long interview process, Modell had whittled the list down to Gregg or Monte Clark, who'd been an anchor on a great Browns offensive line throughout the 1960s. Despite Clark's Cleveland connection and slightly longer coaching résumé, Gregg was offered the job. Fans were optimistic that Gregg's intensity and football background were exactly what the Browns needed to turn things around and get things back to the way they had been.

Things actually got worse before they got better. A lot 'worse, actually. Gregg took over in 1975, and the Browns promptly lost their first nine games, not breaking into the win column until their stunning upset over the 8–1 Bengals in what would be Paul Brown's final game as a coach at Cleveland Stadium. That win represented a turning point, as the Browns went on to split their final four games. Then, after a wobbly start in 1976, they won eight of their last ten to finish 9–5 and nearly qualify for the playoffs. Gregg was named NFL Coach of the Year, having rescued the Browns from their lowest depths and apparently transforming them back into a contender in just two years.

Meanwhile, the Bengals enjoyed an almost identical storyline with their new coach. Paul Brown was in the unique position of naming his own replacement and thought very carefully about who would fill his shoes and where that individual would take his franchise. He'd mulled it over throughout the 1970s, really, as his retirement seemed more and more imminent. Ultimately the choice came down to a pair of his assistants, both of whom had joined the Bengals franchise at its inception as they began their coaching careers in earnest.

The first was forty-nine-year-old Bill "Tiger" Johnson, the offensive line coach, who'd been an All-Pro lineman with the San Francisco 49ers in the late 1940s and 1950s. The second was a brash, silver-haired up-and-comer from California, who in many ways didn't seem to fit on Paul Brown's staff. He'd broken into pro football with Oakland, weaned on a vertical passing game that had defined the Raiders' brash, entertaining style of football. But he'd been successful everywhere he'd coached and, ironically, came with a recommendation from Tiger Johnson. Over the next eight years, Bill Walsh established himself as a creative offensive mind, constantly doodling plays on napkins and developing a style of football that would redefine the game, eventually called the "West Coast Offense."

Brown knew that Johnson believed in his established system and would keep the ship pointed in the same direction. And though Brown had said things over his final few years as head coach that seemed to indicate that Walsh was the heir apparent, he felt that Walsh was a bit emotional, maybe too much so to be a successful coach in the NFL—perhaps not just for the Bengals, but for anybody. In the years leading up to Brown's retirement, Walsh had been a candidate for a few head coaching jobs in the NFL, but each time Brown had done what he could to quash his chances—either for the good of the Bengals or the good of the league, or maybe, in Brown's mind, both.

In perhaps the defining moment of his ownership of the Cincinnati Bengals, Paul Brown made a fateful decision. He thought Bill Johnson would be a better NFL coach than Bill Walsh and tapped Tiger to take his place. Walsh was thrown the bone of a title bump from "quarterbacks coach" to "offensive coordinator," and while he said all the right things, deep down he was both stunned and hurt. "This has caught me completely by surprise," he told a reporter after he heard the news. In Walsh's view, Brown had blocked opportunities for him to escalate his career, then when the time came to reward him for sticking around, Brown had passed him over—and then talked a couple other teams that had Walsh on their short list for head coach out of hiring him.

Enough was enough. Twelve days later, Walsh bailed out, taking the offensive coordinator position with the San Diego Chargers. In his official explanation, Walsh stated, "I've done about all I can do here," and pointed to "a desire to return to my home state" as his primary rationale for quitting. Which, even in a less PR-savvy era, sounded about as believable as "It's not you, it's me." And indeed, Walsh would later frame the situation more like a divorce than a job change. At the time, Brown shrugged his shoulders about it. "You can't argue much with where a man wants to live," he said, knowing full well that ZIP codes had nothing to do with Walsh's departure.

Let's take a moment to ponder what might have been. After a brief stint in San Diego, then two years as the head coach at Stanford University, Walsh landed what at the time seemed like the unenviable position of head coach of the descending San Francisco 49ers. Over the next decade, he transformed them into arguably the greatest dynasty in NFL history, capturing three Super Bowl titles in an eight-year stretch while drafting and developing some of the greatest players ever to walk onto a football field.

All of this could have happened in Cincinnati.

It's easy and understandable to defend Paul Brown. In 1976, who would have bet that Bill Walsh was a wunderkind who would redefine the game? It's not as if there were an outcry when Johnson was selected over Walsh. And let's be honest, Johnson was a safer bet. Had Brown not tapped him to take over, Johnson likely would have become the next head coach of (ironically) the San Francisco 49ers. With his thick black glasses and stern face, he was Barry Goldwater with a whistle, straight out of 1950s football coach central casting. In other words, Tiger Johnson was everything that somebody like Paul Brown thought a football coach should be. Walsh, on the other hand, was essentially an enigmatic hippie from San Francisco in Brown's eyes. It was all well and good to let him run an offense, but God knew what would happen if he took the wheel of an entire team.

Another owner, perhaps less set in his ways and with a bit more understanding about where the game was and where it was going, might have recognized Walsh's potential and seen how that would fit into the future of the game and tapped him to lead the Bengals. But Paul Brown stuck with what he knew, with what had always worked before. As a result, Bengals fans will forever wonder what might have been.

Even the obstinate Brown eventually recognized it. Shortly after Walsh retired from NFL coaching in 1989, he returned to Cincinnati to broadcast a Bengals game for NBC. He had a long conversation with Paul Brown, who admitted that not hiring Walsh as his replacement was one of the biggest mistakes of his life.

Epiphanies notwithstanding, it was a decision that would haunt the Bengals for years. And in big ways.

But at the time, the Bengals were just fine. They picked up in 1976 where they'd left off the year before, cruising to a 9–2 record and a two-game lead over the defending world-champion Pittsburgh Steelers with three games to play. On the brink of elimination, the Steelers came to Riverfront for a Thanksgiving weekend showdown with the stakes clear: a Bengals win would clinch the division crown and all but eliminate Pittsburgh from the playoff picture. Instead of a coronation, it marked the only time in Bengals history that the scheduled time of a game adversely altered the course of a season.

With kickoff set at 4 p.m. instead of the typical 1 p.m. for television purposes, Cincinnati crept to an early 3–0 lead in the first quarter and nursed it through the second. Then, as if nature itself decided to intervene in the Central Division race, at halftime it began to snow—and snow hard. A thick carpet of the white stuff blanketed the Astro-turf, and, accordingly, both offenses slipped, sputtered, and stalled. The Steelers cashed in a Cincinnati fumble for the game's only touchdown in the third quarter, and the single-digit score held up in a 7–3 Pittsburgh victory. Had the game started at 1 o'clock as per usual, the snow wouldn't have begun to fall until well after the game was over—maybe during the Bengals' celebration in the locker room.

Frustrating as the setback was, the Bengals still controlled their own destiny. Sort of. They could clinch the division crown with two more victories, but that would be easier said than done. The following week, the Bengals trekked west to face the 11–1 Raiders on *Monday Night Football* in Oakland, where the Raiders hadn't lost all year. The team that had ended Cincy's season a year before landed another body blow with an easy 35–20 victory that dropped the Bengals into a tie with the Steelers, who held the tiebreaker and only needed a victory over 5–8 Houston in the season finale. They got it, rendering a Cincinnati blowout over the Jets meaningless. Both teams finished 10–4, but Pittsburgh took its third straight division title thanks to a season sweep of the Bengals. Cincinnati, a game behind New England in the wild card race, watched the playoffs on television.

Joining them on the proverbial couch were the Browns, who'd also flirted with the possibility of crashing the playoffs until the final week of the season following the greatest turnaround in franchise history. In his second year at the helm, Forrest Gregg had orchestrated a six-game swing—from 3–11 to 9–5—and it appeared the Browns were back on the straight and narrow.

And so, with both teams apparently well on their way toward a bright future, they collided at sun-splashed Riverfront Stadium to begin the 1977 season. It was, in many ways, the high-water mark for both Bill Johnson and Forrest Gregg with their respective teams.

In a bitter defensive struggle in which neither team topped 300 total yards, the Browns grabbed a 13–0 halftime lead and then held off the Bengals in the second half for a 13–3 triumph. It was their first win in Cincinnati in five years and marked the first time the Bengals had lost a home opener. Art Modell scurried around the Cleveland locker room afterward like a kid on the last day of school, hugging anyone he could find and calling it the biggest win since the Browns won the NFL title in 1964. While Modell had once again fallen victim to a hyperbolic frenzy, the guys in the orange helmets and pants had immediately established themselves as a genuine contender for the playoffs. And for the next few weeks, they were.

The Browns sprinted to a 5–2 record and stood atop the division at the season's midpoint. But storm clouds had begun to gather. The Bengals delivered some payback with a 10–7 win at Cleveland Stadium in Week Eight—a game almost identical to the opener—that halted the Browns' momentum. The following week, starting quarterback Brian Sipe, who'd finally wrested the job away from 1970 top pick Mike Phipps, broke a shoulder blade against Pittsburgh, and the injury served as a sudden record-needle scratch to the smooth '70s groove the Browns had been jamming to. Since Art Modell had traded away Phipps in the offseason—a trade he'd made without consulting Gregg—the Browns were forced to turn over the reins of the offense to untested Dave Mays, the first African-American quarterback in team history and, bizarrely, a part-time dentist.

With the overwhelmed Mays struggling, the ceiling began to cave in. Players began grumbling about Gregg, who seemed draconian and out of touch—an outlander from the 1960s trying to coach in a different era. Gregg even suspected that there was a spy within the ranks that would report back to the front office anything said in practices and the locker room. He noticed that whenever a team meeting would begin, a clunky heater in the next room would turn off, as if someone wanted to listen in. It may have sounded like post-Watergate paranoia, but in a meeting following another miserable loss, Gregg heard a noise from inside a closet. He yanked open the door, and there stood player personnel director Bob Nussbaumer. Modell, in the role of Richard Nixon in this playlet, fired Nussbaumer and denied any knowledge of the spying activities.

With the tension becoming more and more unbearable, Gregg found a friendly ear in Modell's greatest rival. Gregg talked to Paul Brown as the Browns' 1977 season collapsed around him and admitted he was thinking about resigning. Brown talked him out of it, explaining that that's exactly what Modell wanted him to do. Gregg adhered to the advice for the time being, at least until the walls came tumbling down.

Following a downright obscene loss to Houston in which the Browns committed eight turnovers, Modell sat Gregg down and asked his coach to resign after the season was over. Gregg agreed and settled in for one more week as the lame duck coach of a team going nowhere. But Modell, unable to leave well enough alone, leaked the story (or a version of it) to reporters, who then called Gregg for a comment about his being fired. No, no, Gregg explained, he wasn't being fired. He was resigning. That's not what Modell had told the reporters, and Gregg was steaming. He marched back to Modell and said he'd changed his mind—he wasn't going to resign, he wanted Modell to fire him. So Modell did, on the spot, and assistant Dick Modzelewski served as interim coach in a one-point loss in Seattle in the season finale, a fitting cap to a 6–8 campaign that saw the Browns lose six of their final seven games.

Years later, Paul Brown's wife remembered that just after the news broke of Gregg's firing, her husband told her, "Don't worry. Forrest will be coaching again. We won't let Modell destroy him." And indeed, Brown called Gregg shortly after and welcomed him to the Brotherhood of Coaches Fired by Art Modell.

Bill Johnson's departure from Cincinnati, meanwhile, took a bit longer and was considerably less dramatic, but still remarkably similar. The tough loss to the Browns in the '77 opener initiated a wobbly start to the season that saw the Bengals stumble to a 2–4 record as a struggling Cincinnati offense topped the twenty-point mark just once in the first nine games. But Johnson and the Bengals endured and, with a Saturday afternoon victory over Pittsburgh in the second-to-last-game, pulled into a tie with the Steelers atop the AFC Central. Just like the year before, the Bengals had a division title in their grasp. All they needed was a triumph over the mediocre Houston Oilers in the finale, and they'd clinch the crown and the playoff berth that came with it. Instead, the Bengals fell flat on their faces in the Astrodome, losing, 21–16, and provided the Steelers with the division title wrapped up as an early Christmas present.

For three straight years, the Bengals had been arguably the best team in the AFC Central Division and had been poised to capture the title in

December. Each time, they'd failed. Their window of opportunity had slammed shut, as would become evident in 1978.

For starters, it was a very different team. Four Pro Bowl players had all either retired or been traded away. Partly to appease Paul Brown, who was frustrated by a miserable performance in the first half of the preseason finale, Bill Johnson put quarterback Ken Anderson back into the game to start the second half. Anderson cracked his hand against a helmet on a pass attempt and injured his finger, sidelining him for the first month of the season. Just like when Brian Sipe went down in Cleveland the year before, the Bengals' season immediately slipped into a vortex. They lost all four games Anderson missed—including a painful overtime loss in Cleveland in Week Two in which Cincinnati kicker Chris Bahr missed a chip-shot thirty-seven-yard field goal at the end of regulation that would have delivered a Bengals victory.

Anderson returned in Week Five, but it made no difference, as the Bengals were overwhelmed by the winless 49ers. Paul Brown had seen enough. The following afternoon—just before New York Yankees shortstop Bucky Dent hit a three-run home run at Fenway Park to shatter the Boston Red Sox in a one-game divisional playoff that embellished the Curse of the Bambino—the Bengals announced that Johnson had resigned. Brown named Homer Rice as interim coach to get through the tempest. While Johnson had been a familiar face when he became head coach, Homer Rice was an unknown, even to his own team. He'd been on the payroll for just five months and was probably best known as one of Kentucky's greatest high school coaches. Once again, Brown's coaching choice was a questionable one. If nothing else, it was something of an insult to more established assistants like defensive line coach Chuck Studley, who'd been with the Bengals since the beginning and had already been passed over for the gig once. Not surprisingly, when the season was over, Studley bailed out of Cincinnati to take a job with, naturally, Bill Walsh in San Francisco.

If Brown was hoping the change would stir the Bengals, he was sorely disappointed. They lost the first three games with Rice at the helm, scoring a grand total of three points along the way. A stirring win over the playoff-bound Oilers in Week Nine got Cincinnati off the schneid, but four more setbacks followed, and the Bengals stood at 1–12 heading into

December. The Bengals—and Paul Brown specifically—were showered with criticism, inside and outside the organization. Fans began to think Brown was the root cause, as was the nepotistic front office structure, reflected by assistant GM Mike Brown and director of player personnel Pete Brown. Players grumbled about being treated like meat, and critics accused Brown of being cheap and out of touch. "You won't get Paul Brown adjusting to any social change," said Mike Reid, an All-Pro defensive lineman who quit the Bengals for what became a Grammy-winning career in country music. "He believes he's right and . . . football is all wrong."

At the hub of the criticism was former Cincinnati tight end Bob Trumpy. He'd transitioned into broadcasting after his career was over and was vocal in his criticism of the Bengals on his radio show. When word got back to Brown, Trumpy was fired from his job broadcasting Bengals preseason games. "He does not forgive," Trumpy would say. "He hasn't forgiven me or Art Modell."

But as the team continued to lose, the criticism seemed well founded. *Sports Illustrated* even coined the nickname "Bungles" to describe their comical incompetence. "The simple fact is," *Enquirer* columnist Ray Buck wrote, "the Cincinnati Bengals have become a joke team." Then—kicking off a trend they'd perfect in the 1990s—they put a deceivingly nice cap on an otherwise miserable season. In back-to-back weeks, the Bengals blew out playoff-bound Atlanta, then stunned the 11–3 Rams in Los Angeles with a one-point win on *Monday Night Football*. Best of all, in the season finale, they obliterated the Browns at Riverfront, 48–16.

It was a tough note for the '78 Browns to go out on, since they'd made great strides. New head coach Sam Rutigliano was the anti-Forrest Gregg. He was both personable and creative, opening up the playbook and turning the nondescript Cleveland offense into one of the best in the league. They won their first three games and stood at 4–2 in early October before a rash of inconsistency developed and dropped them under .500. But even with the loss to Cincinnati in the final game, their 8–8 record provided hope for the future.

So did the Bengals' three-game winning streak to close out 1978. But just as they'd do time and again a decade and a half later, the inspiring momentum picked up at the end of one season was lost somewhere between December and September. The Bengals lost their first six games of 1979 before landing a stunning blowout victory over the defending world-champion Steelers. "The first thing I'm going to do," Homer Rice said afterward, "is study the game film to make sure it happened." The levity soon vanished, the Bungles kept bungling, and they stood at 2–10 just before Thanksgiving. The following week, a minuscule crowd of 25,103—the smallest Bengals crowd ever at Riverfront—showed up on a rainy day to see the Bengals slosh past equally terrible St. Louis. They limped into the finale at 3–12, once again hosting the Browns, who this time around had much more to play for.

Rutigliano's second season saw the Browns continue to rise toward the level of playoff contender and establish themselves as the most exciting team in football. They exploded out of the gate with four straight victories—three decided in the final minute and the fourth a blowout over defending NFC champion Dallas on a Monday night. More nail-biters followed, including a fourth-quarter comeback to beat the Bengals in Cleveland and another final-play triumph in Philadelphia. Their propensity for drama earned them the catchy nickname of "Kardiac Kids," and they barreled into the final week with a playoff spot in their sights. The only thing standing in their way was—of course—the Bengals.

While the rivalry had geared down a bit on the field over the previous few years, it had reached new levels that October, when Paul Brown published his autobiography, *PB: The Paul Brown Story*, which was primarily a football manifesto containing his coaching and personal philosophies. *Plain Dealer* columnist Hal Lebovitz called it "one of the most self-serving autobiographies I have ever read." In between the gridiron sermons, Brown did include several anecdotes from his career, and, of course, the most notable dealt with Art Modell. Brown outlined the differences they'd had in Cleveland and some of the shadier details of his firing. But the most damning of his stories about Modell came from Brown's final year, when rookie running back Ernie Davis was diagnosed with leukemia, which would eventually take his life a few months later. Brown said Modell pushed him to let Davis play in a preseason game before a big crowd at Cleveland Stadium. "If he has to go," Modell allegedly said, "why not let him have a little fun?"

NFL commissioner Pete Rozelle fined Brown $10,000 for his harsh words about Modell, who, of course, denied everything. He called the book "libelous and trash." He framed the Ernie Davis episode in slightly better terms, saying that Davis had begged him for a chance to play and his doctors admitted that playing actually wouldn't do any harm. Whomever the readers sided with, any sense of the two men burying the hatchet evaporated the moment the book hit the shelves. Over the remaining years, the need for each man to watch his team beat the other's became something else. While "obsession" might be an overstatement, "compulsion" would not. So even without the Browns' playoff hopes on the line, there was a decidedly more intense mood in each team's front office heading into the final week of 1979.

In a soggy, sloppy finale at Riverfront that saw three failed point-after-touchdown attempts and six turnovers, the Browns controlled the line of scrimmage, nearly doubling the Bengals in total yardage. But the Bengals cashed in on repeated Cleveland mistakes and took a four-point lead into the final minutes. A last-gasp Cleveland drive reached the Cincinnati 5, where, in true Kardiac Kids fashion, the game came down to the final play. A Brian Sipe pass for Reggie Rucker in the end zone was batted away by safety—and future NFL head coach—Dick Jauron, and the Browns' postseason hopes dissolved in the December rain.

Once again, the Bengals had closed out a terrible season by spoiling the Browns' fun. But while the finales of 1978 and 1979 had both been satisfying for the wayward Bengals, Paul Brown knew racking up potshot victories over the Browns wasn't enough. So after Homer Rice and his entire coaching staff were dismissed the next day, Brown made a bold move. In fact, the same one Art Modell had made five years before.

***

Forrest Gregg certainly wasn't selected as the next head coach of the Cincinnati Bengals simply because the Browns had fired him. Paul Brown was too smart to make a move based on an attempt to show somebody up.

Brown, of course, dismissed the connection and any theories that he was trying to humiliate Art Modell by hiring Gregg. "He wasn't picked for anything as far as Cleveland was concerned," Brown said. "That's Mickey Mouse trivia." Cartoon-rodent detail though it may have been, deep down, there had to be a part of Brown that reveled in hoisting up someone Art Modell had casually tossed aside.

It wasn't as if Gregg were in huge demand. After leaving Cleveland, he'd accepted a job as San Diego's offensive line coach but then quit a few months later. He wound up in the Canadian Football League in 1979, coaching the Toronto Argonauts to a 5–11 record. Again, nothing that you'd think would draw the attention of an NFL owner, particularly combined with his 18–23 record as an NFL head coach.

But Paul Brown saw something in Forrest Gregg. Would he have seen it had Gregg had modest success and been fired by, say, the Kansas City Chiefs rather than the Cleveland Browns? Probably. As the Homer Rice era staggered toward its inevitable conclusion in 1979, Brown had been in contact with Gregg, who still had two years left on his Toronto contract. Brown hadn't asked permission to speak with him (a detail that would prove poignant a few years later), but the Argonauts weren't going to stand in Gregg's way once he had a chance to get back into the big tent. Eleven days after Rice was fired, Gregg was named the Bengals' new head coach. By all appearances, the Bengals had started dating the Browns' old girlfriend.

It was a fairly stunning move. Gregg had been the only candidate Brown had talked to (establishing the precedent for the David Shula drive-thru coaching search twelve years later), but he still carried the albatross of the hard-ass reputation he'd built in Cleveland—whispered rumors of three-hour practices, midweek curfews, and telephone bed-checks. Many Bengals were critical of the hiring of Gregg. Mack Mitchell, the only Bengal who'd played under Gregg in Cleveland, stared dumbfounded at the reporter who'd told him the news. "Are you serious?" he asked. Then under his breath, Mitchell whispered, "Oh my God."

Rumors swirled that many players would refuse to play for Gregg, and that he was simply too unreasonable and out of touch to succeed as a coach. Paul Brown always suspected that Art Modell was the one who started those rumors, and he went to Pete Rozelle to complain. "I got fined $10,000 for what I said about Modell in my book," Brown reportedly told the commissioner. "How about getting him to lay off my coach?" Modell, of course, denied everything. "This all sounds like a Paul Brown trick," he said.

With or without the support of his troops, Gregg immediately started to mold the image of his new team. Bringing his offensive line knowledge to the table right away, he endorsed using the Bengals' first-round draft choice on mammoth USC offensive tackle Anthony Muñoz, which turned out to be arguably the greatest draft pick in franchise history. He also assembled a crackerjack coaching staff, starting with a pair of assistants who'd served him in Cleveland—George Sefcik and Dick Modzelewski. He hired a little-known defensive backs coach named Dick LeBeau, who would become a mainstay in Cincinnati for the next two decades and brought in Tulane assistant Lindy Infante, who would help propel the Bengals—and then the Browns—to new heights in the decade to come.

Still, little changed for the Bengals under Gregg on the field as the new decade began. A pair of stunning last-minute victories over the defending-champion Steelers provided some early season excitement. But in general, the offense floundered, and Cincinnati struggled, losing four of its first five games, then five straight heading into late November. The last defeat in the string was the hardest to swallow: a 31–7 spanking in Cleveland, giving the Browns their largest win over the Bengals in their eleven-year rivalry.

That victory marked another red-letter day for the smoking-hot Cleveland offense. Brian Sipe—on his way to NFL Player of the Year honors—threw for more than 300 yards along with four of his thirty touchdown passes for the season as the Browns improved to 8–4. Enjoyable as the rout was, it was uncharacteristic for these Browns that they didn't go down to the wire. The Kardiac Kids had roared back with a vengeance in 1980, with twelve of their sixteen games being decided in the final two minutes, seven by three points or less. The defining moment came in Week Seven, when a last-gasp heave from midfield to receiver Dave Logan with sixteen seconds left pulled out a ridiculous victory over Green Bay.

Though running back Mike Pruitt would top 1,000 yards on the ground, this was a pass-first offense. Sipe threw for a team-record 4,132 yards, with five players catching more than fifty passes. With a one-point comeback win over Pittsburgh in Week Eight and a last-minute triumph in Houston in Week Thirteen, the Browns had suddenly emerged as a contender in the toughest division in pro football. A successful Hail Mary pass by the Vikings on the final play of a Week Fifteen encounter in Minnesota denied the Browns the opportunity to clinch a playoff berth, meaning they'd need a victory in the season finale to clinch both a spot in the playoffs and the AFC Central crown. Almost as if it were scripted, they would find themselves in Week Sixteen in Cincinnati's Riverfront Stadium, where two of their former coaches wanted nothing more than to spoil the Kardiac Kids' storybook ending.

While the Bengals had long since been eliminated from the postseason hunt, there was no doubt that the rematch would be a dramatically more competitive contest than the first meeting in Cleveland. Following that game, the Bengals found another gear. Despite Ken Anderson rotating in and out of the lineup due to injury, Infante had begun taking more control of the offense, and the Bengals started to move the ball freely and put points on the scoreboard. They rolled up more than 500 yards in a one-point win over Baltimore, then notched an overtime win in Chicago the following week to stretch their winning streak to three games and improve to 6–9. For the third straight year, they'd close out the season hosting the Browns, with a chance to knock them out of the playoff chase just as they had the year before. Neither Modell nor Paul Brown had ever wanted to win a Browns-Bengals game more, and now Forrest Gregg added a third layer to this lasagna of bitterness.

The ramp-up to the game only increased the intensity. Rumors swirled that Brown promised his players a special bonus if they won the game, and the Bengals talked about how a win over the Browns would make their season, just as the previous two finales had. The Browns, meanwhile, talked about how long the winter would be if they lost and, deep down, were well aware of the proximity of the panic button. But, as he usually did, Rutigliano kept things loose. In an interview session with reporters in his office, Rutigliano would answer a question, then open up a desk drawer and ask, "Are you listening, Forrest?" With all the backstories, subplots, character arcs, and high stakes, it was a scenario that, author Bill Levy would note, Ernest Hemingway couldn't have written better.

For all the build-up, the game lived up to its billing. The tone was set in the opening minutes when Cleveland safety Thom Darden delivered a wicked blow to Cincinnati wide receiver Pat McInally on a pass over the middle. It was the type of hit for which, three decades later, the litigation-spooked NFL might sentence a guy to life imprisonment. Even in the less-sensitive-to-the-possibility-of-a-head-injury days of 1980, a pall dropped over Riverfront as McInally lay motionless on the field for several minutes. But McInally would leave the field under his own power and eventually return to the game—another move that would land somebody in the stockade in today's NFL.

Sporting a this-is-our-Super Bowl, devil-may-care game plan, Forrest Gregg's Bengals sprinted to a 10–0 lead and were poised to turn the contest into a blowout, à la the final act of 1978. The Browns fought back to tie the game before the half, then Cincinnati safety Ray Griffin—little brother of Ohio State legend Archie—picked off a Brian Sipe pass and returned it fifty-two yards for the go-ahead touchdown in the opening minutes of the third quarter to give the Bengals control once again.

But Sipe and the high-flying Cleveland offense weren't going to be denied. A long touchdown pass to sparingly used receiver Ricky Feacher gave the Browns their first lead late in the period, then the Bengals bounced back to knot the score again when McInally struck back at the Browns with a fifty-nine-yard touchdown catch. With the game and the rivalry reaching new levels of intensity, emotion and momentum swung through the fourth quarter. The Browns took control at their own 45 with six minutes to play and slowly began marching downfield. When the Bengals finally stopped them at the Cincinnati 5, Don Cockroft put them ahead, 27–24, with a short field goal with 1:25 remaining. Forrest Gregg inserted injured Ken Anderson—who hadn't played all day— and he drove the Bengals to the Cleveland 13 before time expired. For the first time since 1971, the Browns had won the division. And just as had been the case nine years earlier, they'd done it with a victory over the Bengals.

The Kardiac Kids' roller-coaster ride continued into the playoffs, where they hosted the Oakland Raiders in what would go down as one of the coldest games in NFL history. With the windchill hovering at thirty-six degrees below zero, most figured the Browns' cold-weather experience would make the difference. But on a playing surface that resembled marble, nobody had an advantage, and points came at a premium. Despite missing three field goals and an extra point after their lone touchdown on an interception return, the Browns took a 12–7 lead into the fourth quarter. An Oakland touchdown pushed the Raiders back into the lead, and a Cleveland turnover in its own territory with just over four minutes left seemed to spell doom for the home team. But a gutsy fourth-down stop gave the ball back to Brian Sipe and the offense at their own fifteen with 2:22 remaining. Everybody in the ballpark knew what would happen next.

Ignoring the miserable conditions, the Browns quickly skated down the tundra, reaching the Oakland 13 with forty-nine seconds remaining. On second down, Sam Rutigliano had a choice—send out kicker Don Cockroft to attempt the go-ahead field goal, or roll the dice one more time with Sipe and his *Battlestar Gallactica* offense. On a normal day under normal conditions, Rutigliano might have chosen differently. But with Cockroft struggling with the whoopsy-daisy surface and the offense on a roll, the coach doubled down on the league MVP.

Sipe's pass wobbled through the arctic wind into the end zone, where, for a split second, tight end Ozzie Newsome had been open. But by the time the ball got there, Oakland safety Mike Davis had changed direction and stepped in front of Newsome to intercept the pass. Game over, season over. The Kardiac Kids had lost in probably the only way they could have.

But it had been an amazing year and extended the upward track the Browns had been on under Rutigliano, improving their record for the third straight year and reaching the postseason for the first time in eight seasons. Expectations were incredibly high for the Browns going into 1981, when the Kardiac Kids would almost certainly continue their spellbinding adventures.

As for the Bengals, that next season was expected to be little more than another rebuilding year. The strong finish to 1980 was nice, but not that different from the false Decembers the Bengals had shown in previous years. If Forrest Gregg really had his act together and the stars aligned, maybe the Bengals could claw to the .500 mark. But they were still a long way off from even being considered contenders for the division title, let alone the Super Bowl.

For both franchises, 1981 changed everything.

***

Even when things were going well in the mid-1970s, the Bengals were considered a fairly bland franchise.

From their grandfatherly coach and owner to their antiseptic, cookie-cutter stadium, there was little noteworthy about them. Even their home city was perceived as staggeringly average, reflected by its selection as the Anytown, USA, backdrop for the hit TV series *WKRP in Cincinnati*.

But nothing mirrored the Bengals' blandness more than their uniforms. They dressed like the bankers of the NFL: plain black-and-white jerseys with plain white pants. And plain orange helmets that made the Browns' lone brown-and-white stripe down the middle look cutting edge. The only thing that made the helmets distinguishable from a generic headset that just rolled off the assembly line were the thin black letters arched along each side spelling "Bengals." As the psychedelic '70s boogied on, the league encouraged the Bengals to create a more vibrant visual identity, and Paul Brown agreed. In addition to the uniforms' white-bread blandness, even he admitted that, from a distance, the Bengals looked a lot like the Browns. "That must have been the last straw," the *Enquirer*'s Tim Sullivan wrote. "The last thing Paul Brown wants to do is publicize Art Modell."

The process of designing and selecting a new look took more than a year, and the news that the Bengals were getting a serious makeover was announced a week after Ronald Reagan was elected president in November of 1980. But its impact wasn't really felt until the following spring, when the Bengals unveiled the new uniforms. And right from the get-go, it was clear these were not just any new uniforms. It was akin to the new president walking into the Rose Garden with a mohawk.

They were unlike anything anyone had ever seen. The jerseys and pants alone provided enough envelope pushing to keep old-school

Cincinnati talking for twenty years: an assortment of black stripes strewn across orange flourishes around the shoulders and down each leg. But that wasn't truly what made Cincinnatians hold their hands over their mouths.

It was the helmets. Good God, the helmets.

The good ol' fashioned "Bengals" lettering was gone, replaced by stripes that seemed to have been laid onto the helmets from above like wet socks being put on the line to dry. They were supposed to represent the stripes going down the back of a tiger—though with the anatomical switcheroo, they'd been shifted to the head. Some people compared them to tire tracks—a fitting analogy considering the Bengals' recent fortunes.

Brown himself had selected the design, which was the most dynamic of the concepts. And for all the NFL's nagging of Paul Brown about sprinkling some made-for-TV eye candy onto his team, there were rumors that even the league brass thought this was too much. The *Cincinnati Enquirer* said the new uniforms made the Bengals look like they were "decked out for the disco," creating a look that was "part strobe light, part jungle, part circus, and entirely different." Believe it or not, Paul Brown admitted that they'd considered going with these uniforms when the franchise began play, which actually would have made sense in 1968, a year essentially sponsored by LSD. But he'd ultimately vetoed the idea—less because they represented such a visual trip to crazytown than because he figured there was nothing worse than a bad team with a crazy uniform. And he may have been right—such a uniform scheme might have defined and weighed down the Bengals in their early years, maybe even thwarting their rapid growth.

But now, thirteen years in, the Bengals were back in an expansion phase, toddling through three straight seasons of ten or more defeats. If they stumbled to another Bungle-like start, would their commitment to stripy-ness turn them into a comedy act? Fifteen minutes into the season, it sure looked like it.

The Bengals were simply dreadful in their opening-day contest with Seattle at Riverfront. Ken Anderson completed only five of fifteen passes and threw a pair of interceptions, one of which was returned for a touchdown as the Seahawks roared to a 21–0 lead going into the second quarter. Forrest Gregg benched Anderson and inserted the curiously named Turk Schonert, who promptly fumbled the first snap of his NFL career. At the depths of their considerable incompetence in 1978 and 1979, the Bengals hadn't been *this* bad. Clearly, it had to be the stripes.

As fans booed and wondered how they could get the old uniforms back, the Bengals slowly made a game of it. They cut the deficit to 21–10 at the half, and with the Cincinnati defense—the league's worst just two years before—stopping Seattle cold, Schonert guided the offense to ten more points in the third quarter. A short Pete Johnson touchdown run in the fourth gave the Bengals a 27–21 lead they would not relinquish, and they wrapped up the biggest comeback in franchise history. Maybe those crazy stripes weren't so terrible after all.

Going into Week Two, Forrest Gregg had a very tough choice to make: stick with Schonert, who'd just led the historic comeback, or go back to veteran Ken Anderson, who'd been the heart of the franchise for nearly a decade. Either choice would have been justified, and depending on how things turned out, either could have been decried as moronic. Gregg handed the reins back to Anderson in what might have been the greatest coaching decision in Bengals history.

Anderson led his own comeback at Shea Stadium, rallying the Bengals from a 17–3 second-quarter deficit to a one-point win over the Jets. Following a Week Three loss to the Browns in Cincinnati—in which Cleveland rolled up 185 rushing yards and controlled the football for more than forty minutes of the game—the Bengals pulled off yet another comeback. Trailing 21–10 in the fourth quarter in Buffalo, Anderson threw a pair of his three touchdown passes—to go along with 328 yards—to force overtime, where the Bengals prevailed and moved to 3–1.

From that point on, dramatic comebacks were unnecessary. All the potential young talent buried within the roster—reflected by the eleven first-round draft choices Gregg had inherited when he took over—had finally been unearthed and come together. With Anderson and the Cincinnati offense rolling—and Lindy Infante directing the show after being promoted to offensive coordinator—the Bengals won nine of their last eleven games. A blowout win over the Steelers in mid-October declared Cincinnati to be a genuine factor in the AFC Central race, while another washout over a strong Chargers team in San Diego suggested that the Bengals just might be the best team in the AFC. Two weeks after that, they rolled up a franchise-record 571 total yards—396 from Anderson through the air—in another easy victory over Denver. Where had these wonderful striped helmets been all these years? Even the players could feel the mojo. "The pumpkin helmet is dead," tackle Gary Burley said after the win over the Steelers. "It's the stripes!"

The fun even carried off the field. Rookie wide receiver Cris Collinsworth appeared on the cover of *Sports Illustrated*—becoming the first Bengal to do so—sporting the new threads and helmet. With his colorful personality and ability to "drop a quote as well as he could catch a pass," according to *SI*, Collinsworth seemed to best personify the swagger of these new Bengals.

Basking in this newfound glory, reenergized fans initiated a chant made up of some grammatical gymnastics that made every English teacher who heard it want to sit on the floor and cry. Someone would articulate the question, "Who they think gonna beat them Bengals?" Others would respond, "Nobody!" To help informalize things a bit, the "they" was shortened to "dey," and in time, the new battle cry simply became a two-word declaration: "Who Dey!" Local brewery Hudepohl capitalized on the team's success (and the serendipitous coincidence of the exclamation being reflected by the first two syllables of its own name) and released "Hu Dey" beer for fans to guzzle down during Cincinnati victories.

The Bengal Express rolled into Cleveland Thanksgiving weekend, where the roles had completely reversed since Cincinnati's last trip north a year before. The Kardiac Kids had fallen on their faces in 1981, finding ways to lose close games instead of winning them. Haunted by injuries and critical mistakes, the Browns slipped beneath the .500 mark for good at midseason and had lost all the momentum they'd built over the previous three years. Their only hope now was to try to spoil the Bengals' season just as they'd spoiled Cleveland's in recent years. No such luck. On a dark, damp Sunday, the Bengals cruised to a 28–7 halftime lead and wrapped up a 41–21 blowout triumph that all but clinched their first playoff berth in six years. On Art Modell's playground, to boot.

The other shoe dropped two weeks later for the Bengals in Pittsburgh, where a goal-line stand with less than a minute to play preserved a 17–10 win over the Steelers that clinched the division crown. Forrest Gregg was carried off the field—an image that simultaneously delighted Paul Brown and haunted Art Modell. Cincinnati steamrolled into the playoffs with a 12–4 record and home-field advantage throughout. Modell and the Browns—licking their wounds after a miserable 5–11 campaign— could only watch and wonder what might have been.

Unlike the Kardiac Kids of the year before, the Bengals avoided a first-round exit. Though they played with fire in the divisional playoffs, allowing Buffalo to rally from an early two-touchdown hole to tie the contest in the fourth quarter. An Anderson-to-Collinsworth scoring pass gave the Bengals the lead for good, and a final Bills drive stalled at the Cincinnati 20 with three minutes left. After three failed attempts, the Bengals finally had their first postseason victory. They'd now host the AFC Championship the following week against San Diego, which had advanced past Miami in an epic overtime affair at the Orange Bowl. Already running on fumes, the Chargers were doomed before they ever took the field at Riverfront.

January 10, 1982, was the coldest day on record in Cincinnati history. Topping the dangerously frigid conditions in Cleveland for the Browns-Raiders playoff game the year before, the Bengals and Chargers faced a gametime temperature of minus nine degrees and a Siberian windchill factor of fifty-nine degrees below zero. Though the sun sparkled brightly overhead, steam hovered eerily over the Ohio River. The entire scene took on a surreal backdrop, and the game would forever be remembered as the "Freezer Bowl."

While the conditions were miserable, the Bengals were unaffected, racing to a 10–0 lead in the first quarter. San Diego narrowed it to 10–7, but quarterback Dan Fouts, struggling with the high winds, threw a pair of costly interceptions to halt promising San Diego drives in the second quarter. From then on, it was all Cincinnati, which scored seventeen unanswered points through the frosty atmosphere and coasted to a 27–7 triumph. At game's end, Forrest Gregg was once again hoisted atop his players' shoulders and carried off the field, and Paul Brown watched from the owner's box with a smile pasted on his face. His Bengals—just a year removed from a string of three straight bungling seasons and a 60-to-1 shot at the season's outset—would wear their new stripes in the Super Bowl. Or, as many writers began calling it, the "Striper Bowl." Brown's fifteen-year journey of creating this team had reached its apex, and when Ken Anderson hugged him in the locker room afterward, the magnitude of the moment overwhelmed him, bringing him to tears.

However much it tore up Art Modell inside to see Paul Brown and Forrest Gregg reach football's ultimate stage before he did, he was graceful about it. At a Super Bowl party just before the game, Modell spotted Gregg's wife and hugged her, explaining how happy he was for her husband and how he'd always known he was capable of this type of achievement.

But while Modell was going out of his way to stamp out any notions of regret for letting a former coach get away in the ramp-up to Super Bowl XVI, Paul Brown was doing the same thing. Waiting for the Bengals were the equally upstart San Francisco 49ers, who'd jumped from 2–14 in 1979 to 6–10 in 1980 to 13–3 in 1981—a massive leap for football mankind. And it had been directed by the man who probably should have replaced Paul Brown on the Cincinnati sideline six years earlier.

It would take a few more years—and a few more Super Bowl titles—before people started flinging the "genius" stamp at Bill Walsh, but the speed at which he'd flipped the 49ers from laughingstock to powerhouse was the talk of football. True, Paul Brown could point to Forrest Gregg's two-year salvage job as evidence that he'd eventually (after a pair of unfortunate missteps) gotten his man. But during the two-week media circus leading up to Super Bowl XVI, many wondered what might have been had Walsh gotten the Bengals job. By the time the magical 1981 season rolled around, would Cincinnati have been in the middle of its own dynasty?

Again playing diplomat, Walsh insisted there were no hard feelings or bitterness toward Brown or the Bengals. Keeping a low profile prior to the Super Bowl, Brown agreed that there was no feud between them, but it was difficult not to believe that he very badly wanted to quash all the "what-ifs" by beating Walsh. And Walsh, those close to him felt, just as badly wanted to beat the Bengals to show Paul Brown what he could have had—just as he'd done with an easy 21–3 49ers victory over the Bengals at Riverfront in early December.

For all the intrigue and Shakespearean backstory, the game itself was a bit of a letdown. The Bengals squandered an early opportunity to take control when Ken Anderson threw an interception deep in San Francisco territory after the 49ers had fumbled the opening kickoff. The rest of the first half was all 49ers, as they parlayed Cincinnati turnovers into seventeen points and roared to a 20–0 lead. The Bengals clawed back into the game with a touchdown on the first possession of the third quarter, then late in the period, they drove to the San Francisco 3 with a chance to pull within six points. After a pair of running plays failed to crack the goal line (and with the 49ers only having ten players on the field, to boot), a third-down swing pass to Charles Alexander ended with him tackled inches from the end zone, and a Pete Johnson run on fourth and goal was stuffed at the line of scrimmage. It was an epic goal line stand that turned out to be the difference in the game.

The Bengals did manage to pull within a single score at 20–14 early in the fourth, but the 49ers, directed by then-unknown third-year quarterback Joe Montana, marched slowly downfield and extended the lead to nine points with a field goal with just under six minutes left. Another Anderson interception set up another San Francisco field goal with two minutes to play, and a desperation Cincinnati touchdown in the final minute simply made the game appear closer than it was. The team that would eventually earn the title of "team of the '80s" had its first title. And Bill Walsh had used the Super Bowl to tell Paul Brown, "I told you so."

Would the Bengals have been world champions had they faced another team, one not coached by Bill Walsh? Or, on the other hand, had they simply defeated themselves with five sacks and four turnovers?

For all the hand-wringing about not hiring Bill Walsh—and it potentially costing the Bengals a Super Bowl title—as the following year unfolded, it appeared that it was the Bengals that were building a dynasty and the 49ers that were a flash in the pan. In a season cut short by a fifty-seven-day players strike, the 1982 Bengals picked up where they'd left off, cruising to a 7–2 record and the No. 3 seed in the NFL's expanded postseason "tournament," as NFL commissioner Pete Rozelle insisted they call it.

Hosting a talented New York Jets team in the first round, the Bengals took a 14–3 lead into the second quarter and appeared on their way to another memorable January. But behind an unstoppable running game, the Jets dominated the rest of the way, rolling up more than 500 total yards and forcing four Cincinnati turnovers, including a ninety-eight-yard interception return for a touchdown that sealed the deal midway through the fourth quarter.

Twenty-four hours before the Bengals were erased from the "tournament," the Browns were trounced by the top-seeded Raiders in Los Angeles in a game that made everyone wonder why eight teams from each conference were allowed in the playoffs. Almost from the pregame stretching, it was painfully evident the Browns didn't belong there. Only showing marginal improvement from their 1981 debacle, the Browns managed to go 4–5 in the rotted schedule of the 1982 season and stumbled backward into the right to be emasculated by a far better team.

It was the first time both the Bengals and Browns had ever made the postseason in the same year, something that would happen just one more time after. It reflected a trend that had begun in 1970 and would carry through into the next century—the Browns and Bengals simply couldn't be competitive at the same time. The minute one reached play-off caliber, the other stumbled into mediocrity or worse. They'd rinse and repeat the process again in 1983, when once more Paul Brown made a curious decision that wound up haunting his team.

Over the previous two seasons, the Bengals had developed into one of the best offensive teams in football. With Ken Anderson at his peak and a myriad of weapons like Collinsworth, tight end Dan Ross, and running back Pete Johnson at his disposal, Cincinnati ranked second in the NFL in total yardage in both 1981 and 1982. Helping develop this potent attack was offensive coordinator Lindy Infante, who'd briefly served as the Giants' receivers coach and was trying to salvage his career at Tulane when Forrest Gregg brought him in to coach the Cincinnati quarterbacks in 1980. With his additional influence late in the season leading to a strong finish, Infante was promoted to offensive coordinator the following year, and the rest was history. Even when Bill Walsh was around, the Bengals offense had never been so good.

Naturally, with that success, opportunities came knocking for Infante. The most promising came from the upstart United States Football League as it finished up its first season in the summer of 1983. Initially set up for its games to be played in the spring and summer so as not to directly compete with the NFL until it found its footing, the USFL was successful in luring several current NFL players and a handful of promising college players to its ranks with massive guaranteed contracts and promises of what might be. So when the Jacksonville Bulls called Paul Brown to request permission to speak to Lindy Infante about potentially becoming their head coach for the 1984 season, Brown knew they were serious. And, unlike the graciousness shown to him by the Toronto Argonauts when he came calling about Forrest Gregg three years before, he denied their request.

Which was, of course, just a formality. They nevertheless spoke with Infante without Brown's permission and offered him the job. Infante accepted, with the understanding that he'd continue to coach the Bengals' offense through the 1983 season, fulfill his contract with Paul Brown, and then take over as the Bulls' head coach in 1984.

No owner is ever excited about losing a talented assistant. But that's usually the price of building a successful franchise. The good news was that Brown and the Bengals would still get the benefit of one more year of Infante's services before he left. But Paul Brown felt he needed to send a message—though to whom it's not quite clear. As soon as he heard that Infante had agreed to terms with Jacksonville, he fired him and then, to emphasize the point, sued him for breach of contract.

It was a highly questionable decision with very little upside. Even Forrest Gregg was upset by the action, not only because it cost him one more year of having one of the best assistants in pro football directing his offense, but now the Bengals had no offensive coordinator just five days before the start of training camp. And in another strange display of morality, Brown wouldn't allow Gregg to attempt to hire any assistants currently under contract with other teams to replace Infante. He didn't want to leave any other teams high and dry the way Jacksonville had done to him (even though Jacksonville never intended to put Cincinnati in an awkward situation—it was Brown who created his own problem by refusing to accept Infante's services for one more year).

Paul Brown had become a moral rebel without a cause, and the Cincinnati offense had become an orphaned unit without a leader. With his options self-limited, Brown promoted tight ends/special teams coach

Bruce Coslet to offensive coordinator. And while Coslet would eventually find his footing and become a highly respected coordinator in his own right, he wasn't there yet.

With the offense "in pieces," as Gregg admitted, the Bengals were dreadful to start the season. They failed to score more than ten points in any of the first three games as Cincinnati limped to a 1–6 start that crippled what became a 7–9 season—dipping the Bengals to third in the AFC Central. Their offensive ranking tumbled from No. 2 to No. 14, and they scored, on average, roughly one less touchdown per game than they had the previous two years with Infante at the helm. Other factors were involved in the Bengals' slip, but it's safe to say things would have been better had Brown let Infante finish out the year.

But Infante wasn't the only one jumping ship. Tight end Dan Ross and receiver Cris Collinsworth—both huge parts of the Cincinnati offense during their rise—agreed to futures contracts to join the USFL when their Cincinnati contracts expired: Ross after 1983 and Collinsworth after 1984. While the news undoubtedly steamed Brown's vegetables just as Infante's impending departure had, he didn't immediately kick Collinsworth and Ross out the door as he did Infante. And it was a good thing he didn't, since they combined for 1,600 receiving yards and eight touchdowns between them in 1983.

Still, it underlined a recurring problem—that the USFL seemed to be targeting the Bengals for offers. Dave Lapham, Jim LeClair, and Tom Dinkel had all jumped from the Bengals to the USFL in the previous seasons, and people began to wonder if the upstart league was leveraging Paul Brown's cheapness or stubbornness to lure frustrated players to greener pastures. And maybe Brown's crusade against Infante was less an attack on him than a misguided reaction to what the USFL was doing to his franchise.

While Ross did bounce over to the new league, Collinsworth never actually made the jump. He was deemed "uninsurable" by his new team, the Tampa Bay Bandits, due to an ankle injury suffered in 1984. He re-signed with the Bengals and played in all sixteen games in 1985, amassing 1,100 yards and making Tampa Bay's decision look almost as strange as Brown's to let Infante go. Collinsworth played the final four years of his career in Cincinnati, saving Brown some face, and the USFL folded in 1986 amid plans to go up against the NFL in the fall, eliminating a thorn from Brown's side.

But throughout 1983, the hits just kept on coming. The same week that Collinsworth announced his intention to shed Bengal stripes, two of the Bengals' better players—defensive end Ross Browner and full-back Pete Johnson—testified in court as witnesses for the prosecution that they'd purchased cocaine, more than fifteen times each, from a Cincinnati plumber. They were eventually suspended for the first four games of the season, and Brown stewed in disgust at what pro football was becoming.

But the biggest blow came six days after the season ended. The Green Bay Packers fired head coach Bart Starr after nine unremarkable years that followed a legendary career as Packers quarterback. Evidently wanting to stick to the same formula that didn't work, they scrolled down the list of former Packers greats from the Lombardi glory years and targeted Forrest Gregg as the optimal replacement. They offered a higher salary and a longer contract, plus more power over player person-nel. Despite the wild and immediate success he'd enjoyed in Cincinnati, it was an offer Gregg wasn't going to pass up, and—in a startling reversal of his handling of the Lindy Infante episode—Brown didn't try to stop him, even though Gregg still had another year left on his contract. The justification, Brown would say, lay in Gregg's long relationship with the Green Bay franchise (and perhaps the fact that that the Packers hadn't been bleeding the Bengals dry over the previous few years). Gregg was released from his Cincinnati contract and on Christmas Eve accepted the job in Green Bay. It was slightly less ugly than his departure from Cleveland six years earlier, but just as stunning.

Unlike the immediate turnaround success he'd enjoyed in both Cleveland and Cincinnati, Gregg couldn't raise the bar in Green Bay. After back-to-back 8–8 records in his first two years, the Packers slipped to 4–12 in 1986—their worst mark in nearly thirty years—and then 5–9–1 in 1987. After the season, Gregg received another sentimental coaching offer, this one from his alma mater, Southern Methodist, which had just been clobbered with the "death penalty" sentence by the NCAA for numerous recruiting violations. Rather than entering a situation loaded with expectations, he'd essentially be building a new program from scratch. After three tours of duty in the NFL, that sounded refreshing. Once again reading the writing on the wall, Gregg left the Packers, who, in a bit of almost comic irony, hired Lindy Infante to replace him.

But not knowing that Forrest Gregg's best days as an NFL coach were behind him, the Bengals appeared adrift as 1983 gave way to 1984—a meandering ship still sailing but filled with holes. Put it all together, and 1983 turned out to be one of the worst years in the history of the Bengals. Not only had their window of opportunity for a title apparently closed, but now they had all kinds of internal strife to handle. Which made them not all that different from the Browns.

Despite finishing '83 with a winning record and just barely missing the playoffs, the Browns went into the offseason with their future bent into a question mark. With many of their primary characters aging or shipped away, the Kardiac Kids era was over, symbolized by Brian Sipe's much-ballyhooed leap to the USFL at season's end. They'd had their own drug problems, symbolized by 1980 first-round draft pick Charles White, who saw his career derailed by cocaine. In fact, drugs had filtered so deeply into the locker room that the team took action. Art Modell supported the formation of Inner Circle, an internal drug response and support team to help players admit their problems and take the first steps toward recovery.

With both the Browns and Bengals facing uncertain futures at the midpoint of the 1980s, what happened next came as a surprise to everyone. Rather than limping through the remainder of a turbulent decade, the next few years would mark one of the most exciting periods in the history of both teams, as well as the golden era of the Browns-Bengals rivalry.

6

Trading Places

2003-2008

It was like *Freaky Friday*, only without Jodie Foster. Or Lindsay Lohan. Though no one knew it at the time, there was a specific moment in 2003 at which the Cleveland Browns and Cincinnati Bengals switched roles. In this course-correcting flash point, the new Browns became the old Bengals, and the old Bengals became . . . well, the old Browns. And each team would actually maintain its stranglehold on that new identity longer than its predecessor had.

As in both versions of the same terrible Disney movie, the supernatural substitution can be pinpointed to one particular afternoon—in this case, to one game. One quarter, really. Arguably, one play.

On September 28, 2003, both the Browns and Bengals appeared to be heading in the same direction they'd been pointed over the previous few years. To the surprise of no one, the Bengals had staggered to their fourth 0–3 start in five years. Meanwhile, the Browns had bounced back from tough losses in the first two weeks of the season to capture a dramatic comeback victory in San Francisco in Week Three that put them back on track to reach the lofty expectations that had set sail after their brief playoff appearance (and subsequent collapse) eight months before.

The teams met at sold-out Cleveland Browns Stadium on an overcast autumn afternoon with their trending patterns expected to continue.

The one wrinkle—that, as it turned out, would define each team's season—was that each team's starting quarterback was living in the huddle on borrowed time. Tim Couch had been supplanted by backup Kelly Holcomb in training camp but was thrust back into the lineup after Holcomb broke his ankle in San Francisco while leading the afore-mentioned comeback. The Bengals, meanwhile, under new head coach Marvin Lewis, had wisely entered 2003 with the plan of nurturing top draft pick Carson Palmer into the starting quarterback role rather than throwing him to the wolves immediately as they'd done with Akili Smith four years before. Veteran Jon Kitna was still slotted to remain the starter for the year, allowing Palmer to absorb, adjust, and not get him-self killed. But after three subpar performances by Kitna in Cincinnati's three losses—extending the Bengals' historic string of incompetence to seventeen defeats in nineteen games—the drums of discontent began beating along the Ohio River. What was the point of sticking with Kitna if the Bengals were mired in another of their patent-pending 3–13 sea-sons? Why not throw the shiny kid from Southern California out there instead of paying him to hold a clipboard for a year? Lewis had deftly sidestepped the issue thus far, but one more loss and he may have had no choice but to toss Palmer to opposing defenses like a Christian to the lions.

And 0–4 became visible on the radar when the Browns scored an instantly demoralizing touchdown on the second play of the game. Instead of folding as they had countless times since Paul Brown's pass-ing twelve years earlier, the Bengals showed pluck. They converted four times on third down on the ensuing drive, which ended when Kitna hit third-year wideout Chad Johnson for the game-tying touchdown. The Browns surged ahead again in the second quarter, and it appeared they'd take the lead into the intermission. But the Bengals drove eighty yards in the final minute of the half and tied the game once again, this time on a fifty-five-yard Kitna-to-Johnson touchdown pass. Something unusual was happening, especially when the Bengals kept the momentum with another eighty-yard drive to open the third quarter, taking their first lead of the game—and the season—on Kitna's third touchdown pass of the day. Even with star running back Corey Dillon sidelined by injury in the second half, the Bengals remained in the driver's seat.

The Browns would spend the rest of the day getting flagged for knucklehead penalties (eleven, for a whopping 101 yards) and squandering scoring chances, several because of all-too-familiar Couch mistakes. Three times they drove into Cincinnati territory, and three times they failed to score, the last when Couch threw a face-palming interception at the Bengals' 28 with a minute left. Kitna knelt out the final seconds, and the teams had identical 1–3 records. And new personalities.

The win bought Kitna more time, and with it he led arguably the greatest turnaround in Bengals history. Cincinnati won seven of its next nine games to vault into contention in the AFC North, beating all three division rivals along the way. The resurgence peaked with a stirring victory over a 9–0 Kansas City team, a triumph that the vocal Chad Johnson had guaranteed, Joe Namath-style. A dozen years of misery had dissolved in the franchise's first enjoyable season since the Who Dey heyday of the 1980s. They entered the final week not only with a chance to post their first winning record since Carson Palmer was in fifth grade, but with a shot at a playoff spot and/or the division title.

The only thing that could spoil it were the wheezing Browns, who'd spent the rest of 2003 tripping over their own feet time and again. In the middle of the turmoil, they abruptly released their best receiver, Kevin Johnson, citing an attitude problem in a whiplash-inducing roster move reminiscent of Bill Belichick pink-slipping Bernie Kosar ten years earlier. And as with seemingly all bad teams, there was drama at the quarterback position, as the Browns alternated back and forth between Couch and Holcomb as if comparing paint swatches. They staggered into the finale at Paul Brown Stadium at 4–11, having lost eight of their last nine games, with nothing to play for—not even their pride, which had long since caught a flight home.

Considering the odd history of the teams and their inexplicable tendency to carpet-bomb each other's storybook seasons, you can guess what happened next.

Against expectation and any semblance of common sense, the Browns controlled a game that the Bengals had every reason to win. Just as the Bengals had done in their first meeting, the Browns endured a first-drive Cincinnati touchdown that was usually enough to send them spiraling toward defeat. Propelled by unheard-of fourth-round draft pick Lee Suggs, the Browns surged into the lead just before the half. Suggs, who'd carried the football a grand total of thirty times during his rookie season going into the finale, broke free for a seventy-eight-yard touchdown run just before the half, then bounced around left end for a twenty-five-yard score that gave the Browns the lead for good early in the fourth quarter. He'd wind up with 186 yards on the day, the best tally by a Cleveland running back in nineteen years.

Trailing by eight points in the final minute, the Bengals saw their last-gasp drive end—just as the Browns' last-gasp drive had ended in September—with an interception. The beat-down Browns had torpedoed Cincinnati's feel-good season and ensured the Bengals' thirteenth consecutive nonwinning record.

Still, the franchises' trajectories had shifted. And yet, ironically, both teams essentially rinsed and repeated the exact same season the following year. The Browns once again split their first six games, including a 34–17 thumping of the Bengals in Cleveland, while the Bengals—now with Carson Palmer at the wheel and unhappy franchise running back Corey Dillon traded away—dropped four of their first five. Just like the year before, both teams made a U-turn in late October and headed in opposite directions to the finish line. Cincinnati won seven of its final eleven to finish 8–8 once again (a fourteenth straight nonwinning season, for those keeping score at home), while the Browns imploded with a nine-game losing streak that defined a woeful 4–12 campaign.

In the middle of the teams' antithetical paths to the finish line, they collided in one of the batshit craziest games in NFL history. One that, even more so than the 2003 finale, lacked a single kernel of common sense and seemed to stretch the parameters of football logic to the breaking point. It was, in retrospect, almost as if something supernatural had possessed both teams for three hours on a November Sunday in Cincinnati.

As the Browns began their moribund losing streak, the initial thing to go was whatever marginal offensive competence they had in the first place. Officially giving up on Tim Couch, for the first of what would prove to be several times, the Browns turned to the scrapheap of preowned starting quarterbacks, hoping to find secondhand salvation. After twice leading the San Francisco 49ers to the playoffs, Jeff Garcia was tapped to do the same with a Browns team that still had glimmers of hope going into 2004. As it turned out, Garcia was average at best, then essentially lost for the season in Week Ten with a separated shoulder. Even before turning back to Kelly Holcomb, Tim Couch's understudy in frustration, the Cleveland offense had begun to dissolve, managing to score a total of just thirty points in its first three games of November and failing to accumulate more than 230 total yards in any of the three.

The Bengals' offense had been nearly as offensive the week before, managing just over 200 yards in a loss at Pittsburgh that dropped them to 4–6. Whatever would happen on that Thanksgiving Sunday at Paul Brown Stadium, it didn't figure to be entertaining. Instead, somehow, the Browns and Bengals put on one of the finest offensive displays in the history of football.

They each scored touchdowns on their first possessions, and a long Palmer-to-Chad Johnson scoring pass on Cincinnati's second series gave the Bengals a 14–7 lead before the game was five minutes old. With the offense humming at a blast-furnace level not seen in nearly two decades, the Bengals watched their lead swell to 27–13 at the intermission of what had been a wild first half. But most of the crazy was still in the box.

In the second half, maligned Kelly Holcomb and the woebegone Cleveland offense went straight-up video game on the Bengals. After managing only three touchdowns over the previous month, the Browns scored touchdowns on their next five possessions, including four scoring passes from Holcomb, who'd thrown just two over the previous calendar year. Though the Bengals managed to throw some points on the board in between, their comfortable lead evaporated, and the Browns held a 48–44 margin with ten minutes to play. Fittingly, the Bengals surged back ahead with a touchdown on their next possession—their sixth— and the Browns would have one final shot, regaining possession at their own 17 with two minutes left. After picking up a first down, Holcomb's next pass was picked off by Cincinnati defensive back Deltha O'Neal and returned for the game-clinching touchdown in a 58–48 Cincinnati triumph.

The 106 combined points—from a pair of teams averaging a

combined total of thirty-six per game going into the contest—were the second-most ever scored in an NFL game. The teams' previously asthmatic offenses had combined for more than 960 total yards, including 413 passing yards and five touchdowns by Holcomb and 202 yards on the ground by Cincinnati running back Rudi Johnson.

Symbolically, the Cincinnati victory gave the teams identically miserable 29–62 records since the Browns had returned in 1999—the worst mark in the league. From that point forward, the Bengals would never again trail the Browns, as the trend that had begun with the teams' burlesque *Freaky Friday* routine the previous September hit cruising altitude.

The 58–48 carnival show was an utterly preposterous game and, fittingly, had an equally bugnuts coda. Two days later, after pointedly refusing to resign under pressure from the front office the previous week, Browns Head Coach Butch Davis abruptly quit. In the days that followed, Davis cited health reasons, admitting that he'd suffered a panic attack the morning before the Bengals game and was afraid he'd have another episode on the sideline. It was a strange thing to confess, especially after such a strange departure and an even stranger finale. But, as *Plain Dealer* columnist Bud Shaw put it, "if you are seriously panicked over playing the Bengals, get out before New England comes to town."

A controversial coach whose legacy had been poor preparation and teams that lacked both focus and basic fundamentals had an emotional flameout just before taking the field at Paul Brown Stadium to lead Paul Brown's now-embarrassing namesake.

Almost as if he'd been confronted by the vengeful ghost of Paul Brown.

***

For as much as long-suffering Bengals fans enjoyed the breakthrough of 2003 and even the steady progress shown in 2004, it was the 2005 season that they'd been waiting for. That's when everything came together in a season that mirrored—and in some ways exceeded—the two Super Bowl campaigns that had preceded it.

It began, fittingly, with a win over the Browns on opening day that set the template for what was to come: sterling performances from Palmer (280 yards through the air), Rudi Johnson (126 yards on the ground), and Chad Johnson (91 receiving yards). All three would enjoy the finest seasons of their careers as the Bengals suddenly became a no-kidding-around title contender.

Playing on slick new field turf that replaced the leaky-septic-tank grass of Paul Brown Stadium the year before, they won five of their first six and seven of their first nine, jousting with the Steelers for first place in the AFC North. A thrilling win in Pittsburgh the first weekend in December put the Bengals in the driver's seat toward the division crown. The wayward 4–8 Browns then emerged in the traditional spoiler role, pushing the Bengals to the limit in Week Fourteen before a last-second Cincinnati field goal ended the Browns' improbable (and, once again, highly illogical) upset bid.

The following week, the Bengals clinched their first division championship in fifteen years with a blowout win in Detroit. They finished 11–5 and would host a first-round postseason game at Paul Brown Stadium.

Like the wedding of a homely relative, it was the game Cincinnati had long been waiting for—and was never quite sure would come. Not only was it an honest-to-God playoff game in the Queen City, but it was against the hated Pittsburgh Steelers, who, not for nothing, had begun a long and revered run of success just as the Browns and Bengals fell apart in the early 1990s. The Bengals were teed up to take out fifteen years of frustration in one afternoon.

The long-overdue enjoyment lasted two plays.

On the Bengals' second offensive snap, Carson Palmer launched a long pass down the sideline for wideout Chris Henry, who reeled it in for a sixty-six-yard gain. The capacity crowd at Paul Brown Stadium roared, as fans sensed poetic justice flowing over them like a wave. By all appearances, this was indeed the Bengals' day.

Then everyone's attention turned back downfield, where Carson Palmer lay on the turf, writhing in pain. The replay—which would be looped again and again and burned into the minds of Bengals fans—showed Pittsburgh defensive end Kimo von Oelhoffen crashing into

Palmer's left knee. It buckled in that way that all longtime sports fans recognize as an indicator of a catastrophic injury. And that's precisely what it was: a torn anterior cruciate ligament.

It was Ki-Jana Carter all over again, but even worse. Of course, quarterbacks get hurt all the time. But *this* quarterback? And on his first pass in the team's first playoff game in fifteen years? Could there be a clearer indicator that you weren't meant to achieve your dreams than to see your star player get injured two plays into one of the biggest games in franchise history? Once again, it felt as if something (or somebody) somewhere didn't want the Bengals to succeed—this time on their most anticipated day and their biggest stage in a decade and a half.

Somewhat lost in the thunderclap of the haunting symbolism of Palmer's injury, the Bengals actually fought nobly. Jon Kitna, who had played a key role in the initial turnaround two years before, replaced the franchise quarterback in the huddle and led the Bengals to scores on their first two possessions to build a 10–0 lead. A field goal midway through the second quarter made it 17–7, and it appeared the Bengals might have just enough chutzpah to pull this off.

But reality eventually settled in. The playoff-seasoned Steelers remained poised and crept back into the game, while the Bengals began to fall apart. A botched Cincinnati field goal attempt on the first possession of the third quarter set the tone for the second half, and the Steelers took the lead with five minutes left in the period. Stymying Kitna—sacked four times with a pair of interceptions—and the now-impotent Cincinnati offense, the Pittsburgh defense held the Bengals scoreless in the second half. The Steelers offense warmed up and scored the game's final twenty-four points in a decisive 31–17 victory. Four weeks later, the Pittsburgh Steelers were Super Bowl champions, and the Bengals were left to wonder what might have been. Or, considering the spooky nature of how Palmer was smitten down, what might never be.

The 2005 Bengals were on par with—some would argue even better than—both of Cincinnati's previous two Super Bowl teams. Especially considering how Pittsburgh was able to maneuver its way to a title, it may have been the franchise's best-ever shot at a championship. And it all disappeared in a puff of knee ligament.

Remarkably, in the face of rumors that the injury might be

career-threatening, Palmer was in the starting lineup for opening day the following season. With Palmer's shredded ACL replaced by one from a cadaver (find the symbolism there if you want), it appeared the Bengals would simply pick up where they left off. They won their first three games, including a blowout victory over the Browns in which Palmer threw for 352 yards and a stirring win in Pittsburgh in which the Bengals enacted some measure of revenge for the indignity of the previous January.

But a blowout loss to the mighty New England Patriots the following week in Cincinnati sent the Bengals into an inexplicable tailspin. They would lose five of their next six, including a one-point loss to an 0–4 Tampa Bay team and an incomprehensible defeat in San Diego in which Cincinnati permitted forty-two points in the second half to squander a 28–7 halftime lead. A four-game winning streak got the Bengals back on track for a second straight playoff bid, which hung in the balance in a Christmas Eve showdown with the also-contending Broncos.

Amid fluffy Rocky Mountain snow flurries, the momentum swung back and forth before the Broncos built a 24–17 lead in the fourth quarter. Taking over at their own 10 with less than four minutes to play, the Bengals drove ninety yards to score a dramatic touchdown with forty-one seconds remaining. Overtime appeared imminent, but on the ensuing point-after attempt, long snapper Brad St. Louis misfired the slippery football and holder Kyle Larson couldn't catch it, resulting in a snowy pileup and a one-point Cincinnati loss. "That only happens in PlayStation games," said Denver—and former Cleveland—lineman Kenard Lang.

Now needing a win and help to sneak into the postseason, the Bengals found themselves in an eerily familiar place in the finale: hosting the Pittsburgh Steelers in a do-or-die game. Cincinnati avoided any ominous portents and surged ahead with a Carson Palmer touchdown pass with less than three minutes to play. But the Steelers once again spoiled the party, quickly driving for the game-tying field goal, then capturing victory two plays into overtime on a sixty-seven-yard Ben Roethlisberger touchdown pass. The Bengals not only failed to return to the playoffs, but had taken a step backward, slipping to 8–8. Their once-lofty title aspirations now appeared wobbly and would fall apart altogether the following September on a trip to—you bet your sweet bippy—Cleveland.

***

While the Bengals had emerged from the cocoon of incompetence as a title-contending butterfly, the Browns had become a bad sitcom.

In the aftermath of Butch Davis's sloppy administration and departure, the Browns set forth on a quixotic quest they'd become so familiar with in the next decade: finding a new head coach. For as scattershot as many of their subsequent experiences would appear to be, this choice was about as solid as it could get. Highly respected Romeo Crennel was lured away from Bill Belichick, for whom Crennel had served as defensive coordinator on three championship Patriots teams.

And there was, if not drastic improvement, then at least some welcome competency right out of the gate. The Browns went 6–10 in Crennel's first season but then dipped back to 4–12 in 2006. The only truly memorable moment of Romeo Part 2 was center LeCharles Bentley—who'd just signed a six-year, $36 million contract—shredding his knee on the first day of training camp, essentially ending his career. Good times, great oldies.

Even under Crennel's leadership, the Browns still couldn't quite settle on a quarterback. The Jeff Garcia experiment became the Trent Dilfer experiment, which then turned into more of a local community outreach program when Northeast Ohio native and Kent State grad Charlie Frye somehow became the starter.

After four straight losing seasons, there weren't exactly high expectations for the Browns going into 2007, but it only took one quarter for the season to apparently fall apart. Looking as if they'd never played the game before, the Browns trailed Pittsburgh 17–0 before fans could even order their second beer. Frye was benched after getting sacked five times on seven offensive series, and the Browns were on their way to a 34–7 thrashing.

In what may have been the most desperately pathetic personnel move in NFL history, Frye was traded away the following afternoon. Giving up on the season wasn't anything new for the Browns, but this appeared to be the fastest instance on record. Derek Anderson—Frye's unremarkable backup—was named the starter for Week Two, and it appeared the second verse would be the same as the first.

Into Cleveland rolled the Bengals, who had defeated the Browns five straight times and were coming off a rousing victory over defending division champ Baltimore. And, just like the previous week, the Browns defense permitted a long touchdown drive on the first series of the game, followed by a bumbling three-and-out by the wayward Cleveland offense. Another blowout appeared imminent.

Instead, the Browns and Bengals reenacted the bizarre fireworks show they'd put on three years before. The teams combined for five touchdowns in the second quarter, including three scoring passes from Anderson, who, in his fourth career start, had somehow become the unlikely gunslinger going eyeball-to-eyeball with Carson Palmer. Anderson threw two more touchdown tosses in the second half, giving him five for the day, and with newly acquired running back Jamal Lewis exploding for 215 yards on the ground—the team's highest tally in forty-four years—the Browns topped the fifty-point mark for the first time in eighteen years and built a 51–38 lead with under six minutes left.

Naturally, the Bengals scored to narrow the margin on Palmer's sixth touchdown pass of the afternoon, then regained possession with a minute left with a chance to pull out a victory. But, just as things had ended in Cincinnati in 2004, the Browns came up with an interception that secured a wild and woolly 51–45 triumph—arguably the nuttiest in team history. "This game," *Enquirer* columnist Paul Daugherty wrote, "was a great reason smart people don't bet on NFL games."

While the total number of points in Crazy Bowl II was slightly behind the initial encounter, the other statistics surpassed it, essentially rewriting each team's media guide. The teams combined for twelve touchdowns, fifty-six first downs, and a ludicrous 1,085 total yards.

Just as memorable as the victory was the aftermath. It lit a fire under the previously lifeless Browns, and they embarked upon their finest season since their return to the NFL. With Derek Anderson inexplicably emerging as a top-notch quarterback, the primarily untapped potential of the Cleveland offense suddenly became lethal. First-round draft picks Braylon Edwards and Kellen Winslow both topped 1,000 receiving yards, and Jamal Lewis rushed for better than 1,300 yards—the best by a Cleveland running back in nearly fifty years. Anderson, meanwhile, threw for 3,700 yards and twenty-nine touchdowns, which was the most by a Browns quarterback since Brian Sipe in the Kardiac Kids season of 1980.

Powered by their at-times-unstoppable offense, the Browns would win nine of their next thirteen games as they emerged as arguably the most exciting team in the NFL. After rallying from a fifteen-point deficit to knock off Seattle in overtime one week, they went down to the final seconds in the following two. First, a long Cleveland field goal fell just short to preserve a Steelers victory in Pittsburgh. Seven days later in Baltimore, the Browns attempted another potential game-tying field goal as time expired. The football hit the left upright, spiraled over the cross bar, bounced off the stanchion holding up the cross bar, and floated back down over the cross bar and into the end zone. Initially the kick was ruled no good, and the Ravens departed the field thinking they'd just escaped with a narrow victory. But replays (and a quick check of the rule book) confirmed that since the kick had crossed the crossbar, it was good, and overtime was in order. The shellshocked Ravens were dragged back onto the field just long enough for the Browns to drive back into Baltimore territory and kick the game-winning field goal—no pinball bounces necessary this time.

It was that kind of season.

After enduring blizzard-like conditions in an 8–0 win over Buffalo in Week Fifteen, the Browns now controlled their playoff destiny. A triumph in Week Sixteen would secure a satisfying postseason berth and underline 2007 as a turning point in franchise history. The only team in their way was—yes indeed—the Cincinnati Bengals.

Never completely recovering from the loss in Cleveland, the Bengals stood at 5–9, their title hopes of the previous two seasons evaporated. Now they were simply playing out the string in what would be their first losing season in five years. But just as they'd done twice to the Browns to close out the 1970s and mirroring what the Browns had done to them four years before, the Bengals had just enough left in the tank to napalm their rivals' renaissance. On a blustery day in Cincinnati, the Browns inexplicably kept insisting on a pass-first offensive game plan. Consequently, Anderson had his worst game of the season, throwing four interceptions as the Bengals built a 19–0 third-quarter lead. The Browns clawed back to within five in the final minutes, but a last-gasp drive ended when an Anderson pass to the end zone from the Cincinnati 29 fell incomplete on the game's final play.

The Browns closed out the season with a win over San Francisco to finish 10–6—their best record in thirteen years—but it wasn't enough to get them into the playoffs. Worse, it marked their last truly enjoyable season to date.

Expectations were understandably high for 2008, but they quickly became hysterical. A "Super Bowl" chant welcomed the team on the first day of training camp, and the Browns had five prime-time appearances on their schedule, more than even the perennial powerhouse New England Patriots, who'd gone 16–0 the previous year. Partially with the weight of unrealistic expectations swirling around them and partially because they were never that talented an overall team to begin with, it took roughly a hot second for the Browns' true colors to emerge.

They were manhandled in their first three games. After an ugly win over also-0–3 Cincinnati, they flashed their potential with a Monday-night rout of the defending-champion New York Giants. But in essence, that would be it for the 2008 Browns. They would lose eight of their last nine games, failing to score an offensive touchdown in their last six.

Not that there weren't entertaining moments on the return flight to noncontention. In training camp, receiver Braylon Edwards suffered a severe laceration on his foot when he was goofily running sprints in his socks and was accidentally spiked by a teammate. A controversy over an unusual number of Browns players coming down with staph infections—two that year brought the total to six in five years—led to a cavalcade of hand-wringing, finger-pointing, the end of a couple of careers, and legal action. Kellen Winslow II was the latest soldier to fall in the Browns' bizarre staph war, and he then accused the Browns of trying to cover up the problem. It led to a screaming match between Winslow and general manager Phil Savage outside the Browns locker room after a loss in Washington.

Savage, whose Richie Cunningham looks masked his Teamster tendencies, was at the centerpiece of another controversy a few weeks later when he responded to a negative email from a fan during a Browns' Monday night game against the Bills. Savage closed out this erudite battle of wits with: "Go root for Buffalo. Fuck you." He apologized but, shortly after, joked about the exchange on a radio show and then proceeded to throw the Browns' coaches under the bus, positing that he'd provided them with enough talent to win.

Along the way down the Mellow Brick Road, the Browns gave up on newly anointed hero Derek Anderson in favor of much-ballyhooed Ohio native Brady Quinn and finished 4–12—the first of what would be six straight seasons of eleven or more losses. A year after being a candidate for Coach of the Year, Romeo Crennel was fired, along with "Fuck you" Phil Savage, and the Browns were, once again, back to the drawing board.

As were the Bengals, who'd suffered through an almost identical 4–11–1 season, peppered by an 0–8 start that brought back memories of the disaster-film campaigns of the 1990s. The most memorable moment of the year took place in August when gadfly receiver Chad Johnson legally changed his name to Chad Ochocinco—reflecting his self-labeled nickname, the Spanish translation of his jersey number. By season's end, most Bengals fans wanted an even more drastic change on the sideline. With vociferous calls for Marvin Lewis's dismissal, the Bengals stood steadfast, and Lewis remained the head coach. And while he was criticized for the decision, Mike Brown would see it pay off.

The Bengals won four of their first five games in 2009, including a marathon victory in Cleveland decided on a field goal on the final play of overtime. They stayed hot, improving to 9–3 in early December, then clinched the division title in the second-to-last week of the season. This unexpected turnaround reenergized the fan base, and Paul Brown Stadium was packed to its budget-busting rafters for a first-round playoff encounter with the New York Jets. While not as soul-crushing as the Bengals' last postseason experience four years earlier, the result was the same. The underdog Jets built a comfortable lead and cruised to a 24–14 triumph.

Just as the Browns would with hiring and firing coaches and quarterbacks, the Bengals had begun to master an infamous tendency that would define their franchise for the next decade: losing postseason games they probably should have won.

Which, perhaps with a pinch of bitter irony, was the signature trademark of both the Bengals and Browns during their rivalry's short but memorable golden era a generation before.

7

Dogs and Cats

1984-1990

The Bengals began the Orwellian year of 1984 by introducing their fifth head coach, the fourth hired by Paul Brown. This one was perhaps the strangest choice of all.

True, pulling Forrest Gregg in off the Canadian tundra was strange. But pulling in Sam Wyche from the Indiana cornfields was stranger.

At least Bengals fans—if not Bengals players—knew who Sam Wyche was. They remembered his stint as Cincinnati's backup quarterback at the dawn of the franchise. He stretched his career over four more seasons with three different teams before finally hanging it up. After running a sporting goods store for a couple of years, Wyche thought he'd try a career in coaching. He applied for a pair of high school coaching jobs and was promptly turned down. Minutes after the second rejection, his phone rang. Bill Walsh, Wyche's old quarterbacks coach and soon to become the symbol of everything that might have been for the Bengals, was taking over the San Francisco 49ers and wanted to know if Wyche would now be *his* quarterbacks coach. Over the next four seasons, Wyche helped develop Joe Montana and the vibrant San Francisco offense that slapped around the Bengals in Super Bowl XVI.

But even before Wyche's stock began to rise, Paul Brown kept his eye on his former quarterback. He and Forrest Gregg had interviewed Wyche in 1980 for the job of Bengals offensive coordinator and eventually offered him the job. But since the 49ers wouldn't let Wyche out of his contract, he stayed in San Francisco, and the Bengals eventually turned to Lindy Infante instead.

Three years later, Wyche was hired to replace Lee Corso as the head coach of Indiana University's long-struggling football program for what proved to be a short-lived tenure. After a Hoosier-typical 3–8 campaign, the Bengals came calling once again. Though his résumé was relatively thin, Wyche was the only person Paul Brown interviewed to replace Forrest Gregg. Four days after Gregg resigned, Wyche—personally recommended by Bill Walsh—was hired as the new head coach of the Bengals. At thirty-eight years old, he was, like David Shula would be after him, the youngest coach in the NFL.

And thus began the wildest—and most entertaining—stretch in franchise history.

It began at his introductory press conference. When asked whether Wyche was hired as a puppet coach who would be beholden to Paul Brown, Wyche leaned forward and said, "What should I say now, Paul?" Rimshot, laughter, and we were off to the races.

Wyche had always been colorful in his time as the Bengals' backup quarterback, pulling pranks and magic tricks while bringing energy to the franchise's toddler years. As a coach, he'd channeled that energy and creativity into his work, and with no oversight to stop him, the next few years would see some truly unorthodox on- and off-field strategies. Some worked brilliantly. Some did not.

As it turned out, Wyche's inaugural campaign of 1984 forecasted the spasmodic mood swings that were to come. Despite holding a second-half lead in their first three games, the Bengals lost each, then two more to fall to 0–5—their worst start in five years. After blowing another fourth-quarter lead in New England in Week Seven, they stood at 1–6, and the Sam Wyche era appeared ready to implode before it had really begun.

Into town came the also-struggling Cleveland Browns, who limped into the game with an identical 1–6 mark. But theirs was even more surprising. After barely missing the playoffs in 1983, the Browns were confident that backup Paul McDonald would seamlessly take the starting quarterback reins from Brian Sipe, who'd departed to join Donald Trump's New Jersey Generals of the USFL. With a defense developing into one of the finest in the game, many felt the Browns would be a bona fide playoff team in 1984. And indeed, as the season began, Art Modell called it the finest team he'd seen since he'd been the owner. Which was his wont to do every couple years.

Yet over the first half of that season, the Browns were dreadful. McDonald completed just eight of twenty-seven passes in his debut as the full-time starter and threw eleven interceptions in the first five games. Playoff hopes were instantly dashed, and suddenly, once-beloved Sam Rutigliano's job was in jeopardy. Considering how much emphasis Modell put on beating the Bengals, it seemed like the Browns' Week Eight trip to Cincinnati might determine if Rutigliano finished the season or not. Everybody knew it, especially Rutigliano. "You could lose football games as a Browns coach," he would write in his autobiography, "but you would not be forgiven if you lost to Cincinnati."

It was, statistically speaking, the lowest point in the history of the rivalry at that juncture. On a fittingly overcast October afternoon, neither team managed to score a touchdown. After trading field goals three times, the game was tied at nine late in the fourth quarter. A long Cincinnati pass pushed the Bengals into Cleveland territory, and Jim Breech booted a thirty-three-yard field goal as time expired to give the Bengals the victory.

Two hours later, Rutigliano was fired.

The victory, sloppy as it may have been, lit a fire under the Bengals, and over the final half of the season, they became one of the hottest teams in the NFL. They won seven of their final nine games, including their last four to claw back into the race in a very mediocre AFC Central. After a blowout win over Buffalo in the finale, the Bengals wrapped up with an 8–8 record and quickly scrambled to the locker room and flipped on televisions. If the 11–4 Raiders could knock off 8–7 Pittsburgh in Los Angeles, the Bengals would take the division crown. But the Steelers—in their final hurrah with the remaining members of the Steel Curtain—pulled off the upset and captured their ninth and final

AFC Central title of the era. The Bengals went into the offseason disappointed, but optimistic for what the Sam Wyche era might hold.

The Browns, meanwhile, also garnered some level of good feeling with the way 1984 wrapped up. Under the steady, close-to-the-vest leadership of defensive coordinator Marty Schottenheimer, promoted to replace Rutigliano, the Browns split their final eight games to finish a much more respectable 5–11. Setting the tone for the future, their defense had developed into one of the best in the league. Led by a strong linebacking corps anchored by All-Pros Clay Matthews and Chip Banks, the Browns ranked second in the league in fewest yards allowed. But the unit was personified by its secondary, specifically cornerback Hanford Dixon, who, with a simple analogy, inadvertently defined the personality of the franchise for the remainder of the century and beyond.

Early in the year, Dixon described the vicious Browns pass rush as "dogs chasing a cat." And to inspire his teammates in their chase, he began barking at them. While the Browns' overall play did little to capture the imagination of their fans, Dixon's barking gambit did. By midseason, fans began showing up to Cleveland Stadium in dog masks and hanging signs perpetuating the canine moniker. The bleachers at the open end of the stadium became known as the Dawg Pound, which soon would become a force with which visiting teams and coaches—particularly Sam Wyche—would have to reckon.

Unfortunately for Wyche & Co, their 1984 momentum didn't carry over to 1985. Once again, the Bengals struggled out of the starting gate, losing their first three games and four of their first five as they fell off the pace in what would prove to be a balanced—if not formidable—AFC Central. While the Bengals struggled early in the season, the Browns roared to four wins in their first six games to take over sole possession of first place in mid-October. And while their defense was once again sterling, it was a handful of fresh faces on the offensive side of the ball that had fans excited.

With Schottenheimer's conservative approach, the primary weapons were first-year running back Kevin Mack—lured away from the USFL—and second-year fullback Earnest Byner. Combining for more than 460 carries between them, Mack and Byner became just the third pair of teammates to rush for more than 1,000 yards in the same season.

But while Mack and Byner were the fossil fuel of the offense, rookie quarterback Bernie Kosar became the face of it.

Personifying a sea change in Cleveland's long-suffering reputation, Kosar, a Youngstown native, stunned the sports world by announcing his desire to play for his hometown Browns. After a dazzling career at the University of Miami that saw him lead the Hurricanes to their first national championship, Kosar would have been one of the top picks in the collegiate draft. The Browns, even after a lousy 1984 season, were too far down the draft board to have a shot at getting him and couldn't find any takers in trade offers. But Kosar found a loophole. Since he'd graduated early, he had an opportunity to make the system work for him. Two months after the collegiate draft, he entered the supplemental draft, where the Browns were able to maneuver into position to select Kosar. And just like that, the Browns had a franchise quarterback. Their plans to ease him into the system were out the window when starting quarterback Gary Danielson went down with a shoulder injury in Week Five. Kosar was inserted into the lineup, and while the pair would alternate throughout the remainder of 1985 based on Danielson's health and Kosar's effectiveness, it was clear that the Browns were now Bernie's team.

A similar change in leadership was occurring in the Bengals huddle— when they decided to have one, that is. Wyche decided to introduce an iconic wrinkle to his offense, which was now led by a new franchise quarterback. After fourteen years, Ken Anderson had reached the twilight of his career, and Cincinnati needed a replacement. Turk Schonert had filled in admirably as Anderson's backup over the previous few seasons, but when the Bengals had the chance to snag hard-throwing southpaw Boomer Esiason out of Maryland in the 1984 draft, they took it. After seeing limited action sharing time with Anderson and Schonert in his rookie year, Esiason emerged as the regular starter in 1985. As the season wore on, the Cincinnati offense became electric—as good as it had been in Anderson's prime in the Super Bowl season of 1981.

With Esiason at the helm, suddenly the Bengals offense was loaded with weapons. Acquired from San Diego the year before, versatile running back James Brooks became a star, tallying better than 900 rushing yards and nearly 600 more receiving. Beefy fullback Larry Kinnebrew

bulled his way to 700 more yards on the ground. Fourth-year tight end
Rodney Holman emerged as a threat with which defenses had to contend. Plus, in addition to Cris Collinsworth—back from the brink of
USFL defection—Cincinnati had landed a fantastic target for Esiason in
the '85 draft with wideout Eddie Brown, who would tally better than 900
receiving yards and a team-best eight touchdowns in his rookie season.
Ironically, Brown had been Bernie Kosar's favorite target at Miami and
had very nearly joined Kosar in Cleveland. To land the top spot in the
supplemental draft, the Browns had agreed to trade star linebacker Chip
Banks to Buffalo. But Banks balked, refusing to report to Buffalo, and
the Bills instead demanded the Browns' first-round pick in the college
draft—which they'd earmarked for Eddie Brown. The Bengals scooped
him up with the thirteenth pick and, over the next seven seasons, he
would become their most dangerous pass catcher.

With his offensive cupboard full, Wyche implemented a quirky strategy he'd toyed with a few times the year before. To try to tire out opposing defenses and prevent them from making substitutions between
plays, the Bengals would frequently skip the huddle (or slip into a variety
of quick-huddle variations) and just rush up to the line of scrimmage as
if racing the clock at the end of a game. The Bengals enjoyed some success and more than their share of five-yard penalties on the defense for
too many men on the field. But many coaches and brass around the NFL
hated the chicanery and would eventually band together to put a stop
to it. For the time being, though, it was quirky and fun, and the Bengals
turned things around by midseason, pulling into an unusual logjam in
which all four teams in the AFC Central stood at 4–5 in early November.

The following week, the Bengals blew past Cleveland, 27–10, at
rainy Riverfront and dropped the Browns a game back, extending their
losing streak to four games. The script was flipped in the rematch two
weeks later when the Cleveland defense dominated the Bengals and the
Browns cruised to a 24–6 triumph in the Cleveland Stadium mud. This
one catapulted the Browns back into first place, a game ahead of Cincinnati. But the Bengals clawed back atop the standings two weeks after
that with a rousing blowout of the mighty Dallas Cowboys in their first-
ever trip to Riverfront. Rolling up nearly 600 yards of offense, the Bengals built a 50–10 lead and cruised to a twenty-six-point triumph over

America's Team. For all their ups and downs, the Bengals had demonstrated there was a playoff team in there somewhere.

The momentum carried over to the following week as the Bengals built a 24–7 lead at Washington, then, true to form, gave up twenty unanswered points to lose to the Redskins. Even worse for Wyche & Co., a Browns victory over Houston guaranteed that the Bengals couldn't surpass the Browns no matter what happened in the final week, since Cleveland had secured a better division record and, therefore, the corresponding tiebreaker. For all their offensive fireworks, the Bengals would once again watch the playoffs on television.

Consequently, the Browns, despite just an 8–7 record, clinched their first division title in five years the following Saturday when Pittsburgh lost to the New York Giants. Cleveland closed out a schizophrenic regular season the next afternoon with a blowout loss to the playoff-bound Jets, finishing an even .500.

Most argued the Browns had no business in the playoffs. At 8–8, they'd become the first team to qualify for the postseason without a winning record (excluding the expanded format for the strike-shortened 1982 season) since 1969 and the first team ever to win its division with just a .500 mark. Still, for all the hand-wringing for the two weeks leading up to the divisional playoffs, it appeared the injustice of the Browns sneaking into the postseason by way of a weak division would be taken care of swiftly and decisively. The defending AFC champion Miami Dolphins awaited the Browns, riding a seven-game winning streak sparked by the best offense and best quarterback in pro football. Dan Marino's Dolphins were eleven-point favorites—a downright laughable spread for a divisional playoff—and most assumed they'd cover the spread easily.

Instead, the Browns dominated from the get-go. Pounding Miami's suspect defense with an overpowering running game, they roared to a 14–3 halftime lead and expanded it to 21–3 when Earnest Byner broke free for a sixty-six-yard touchdown run early in the third period. The Browns appeared on their way to one of the greatest upsets in NFL history. But, as would become their modus operandi over the next few years, they were unable to close it out. Marino got hot and the Cleveland offense stalled, enabling the Dolphins to creep back into the game and finally surge ahead in the final two minutes. It was a heartbreaking defeat, but just an appetizer for what was to come.

In the aftermath of the Miami defeat, Art Modell realized that changes needed to be made for the Browns to take the next step and become a genuine title contender. While the Mack-Byner combination had proved effective, the playoff game had clearly demonstrated that the Browns' offense—the passing game in particular—needed a dramatic boost. To provide that boost, Modell turned to the man who had done the exact same thing for the Bengals five years earlier.

With the demise of the USFL in the spring of 1986, a flood of good talent—both players and coaches—suddenly became available. NFL teams quickly went to work grabbing whatever pieces they could. The Browns were at the vanguard throughout the mid-'80s, landing a handful of USFL players that would play vital roles in the years to come, including Kevin Mack, offensive lineman Dan Fike, receiver Gerald "Ice Cube" McNeil, and linebacker Mike Johnson. They also acquired Frank Minnifield, who would become Hanford Dixon's counterpart in the defensive backfield, as they formed maybe the best shutdown duo in football. But perhaps the most important acquisition the Browns picked up from the shattered remnants of the USFL was former Jacksonville Bulls Head Coach Lindy Infante. After leaving Cincinnati (or rather, being preemptively booted out the door by Paul Brown), Infante had posted a 15–21 record in Jacksonville before being forced out when the franchise merged with the Denver Gold. It wasn't an awe-inspiring achievement, but the experience had made him an even more appealing candidate to take over the Cleveland offense. He was named the Browns' offensive coordinator in February and immediately went to work redefining the run-first, pass-later mentality Schottenheimer had installed with the same option-route system that had turned the Bengals into the toast of Cincinnati.

The year 1986 marked a fresh change of pace for the Browns-Bengals rivalry. For the first time in a decade, both teams posted winning records, and for the first time since 1970, they were the sole contenders for the AFC Central crown.

Cincinnati landed the first punch in a Week Three Thursday-night showdown in Cleveland. With Cleveland Stadium packed to capacity, the Bengals used a methodical, power running attack to blow open a close game in the second half and cruised to a 30–13 triumph. A three-game October winning streak pushed the Bengals to 5–2, alone atop the Central Division, before the Browns caught fire. With twenty-two-year-old Kosar quickly emerging as one of the NFL's finest young quarter-backs under the tutelage of Infante—and a version of the 1963 Kingsmen hit song "Louie Louie" called "Bernie Bernie" invading the radio airwaves in Northeast Ohio—the Browns suddenly had an offense as potent as Cincinnati's.

Kosar's potential was showcased in November when he threw for more than 400 yards twice in three games—first in a Monday-night pay-back victory over Miami, then in an overtime thriller over Pittsburgh that ended with a thirty-six-yard scoring pass to rookie wideout Webster Slaughter. Another overtime victory over Houston a week later gave the Browns a one-game edge over Cincinnati, setting up a showdown at Riverfront in Week Fifteen for the division crown.

It appeared as if it would be a coronation for the Bengals. Their offensive dominance had been downright silly, rolling up better than 400 yards in five straight games, including a muscular performance over playoff-bound New England the week before in which the Bengals tallied 584 yards—including a whopping 300 on the ground. What's more, they'd won ten of their last eleven at home, including four straight over the Browns, symbolized by a blowout victory over a rattled Kosar a year earlier. Hoping to repeat the experience, a local radio station sponsored a giveaway promotion of small, striped cardboard megaphones called "Browns Blasters." It was a clever idea that turned out to be nothing more than a tragic waste of trees.

With nearly every conceivable advantage leaning toward the Bengals, the Browns stunned and silenced the capacity crowd. They took control on the very first snap—a sixty-six-yard completion from Kosar to Reggie Langhorne, setting up the first of four touchdowns. Another long Kosar-to-Slaughter scoring strike built a 17–3 halftime lead, and the Browns never looked back in the 34–3 triumph. Holding Cincinnati to less than half the yardage it had accumulated the previous week, the Cleveland defense completely grounded the high-flying Bengals offense, holding it to its lowest point tally in five years. It was a watershed moment, particularly for both Modell and Infante.

When the proverbial dust settled on the Riverfront carpet, the Browns had captured their second straight division crown. Despite a rousing victory over the Jets in the finale (in which they tallied fifty-two points and better than 600 yards of offense), the 10–6 Bengals couldn't get the cooperation they needed from other teams to sneak into the playoffs as a wild card. For the fourth straight year, Cincinnati participated in the playoffs merely as spectators.

And for the second straight year, Paul Brown watched Art Modell's Browns provide wonderful drama. Having earned home-field advantage throughout the playoffs following a 12–4 regular season, the Browns hosted the floundering Jets team that had been filleted in Cincinnati in the final week of the season. But the Jets, fresh off a resounding win in the wild-card game the week before, had found their mojo and frustrated the Browns all afternoon. A pair of uncharacteristic Kosar interceptions in the fourth quarter enabled the Jets to grab a 20–10 lead with four minutes remaining, and it appeared they were headed for the AFC title game the following week.

But Kosar rebounded, guiding the Browns on two quick scoring drives to tie the game in the final seconds of regulation. Then, with the Cleveland defense suffocating New York, the Browns survived an emotional body blow when they missed a chip-shot field goal that would have won the game on their first possession of overtime. The teams toiled into a second sudden-death session before the Browns persevered in what became the third-longest game in NFL history. With their amazing comeback, they truly appeared to be a team of destiny and for the first time in seventeen years were one win away from the Super Bowl.

Waiting for them on destiny's doorstep—as they continually would in the years to come—were the Denver Broncos. On a dark, cold afternoon, the teams were embroiled in the kind of defensive struggle that Paul Brown would have loved. The Browns broke the game open and appeared to clear their path to the Super Bowl when Kosar hit surehanded receiver Brian Brennan for a forty-eight-yard touchdown pass to put them ahead 20–13 with 5:43 to play. Better still, the Broncos played the ensuing kickoff like a hand grenade and fell on the football at their own two-yard line. Victory, and a trip to the Super Bowl, were within Cleveland's grasp.

Then John Elway tore it free, driving his team ninety-eight yards—three times converting on critical third downs, including a third-and-eighteen—and tied the game with a touchdown strike with thirty-seven seconds remaining. Their momentum crippled, the Browns hobbled into overtime, quickly went three-and-out on their first possession, and watched Elway march downfield once again. The Broncos won on a thirty-seven-yard field goal—that most Browns fans still swear went over the left upright and not through—and went on to the first of three severe Super Bowl beatings in the Elway era.

For as difficult as the finish was, Browns fans were primed for a new golden era. In just over two years, Marty Schottenheimer had transformed them from one of the worst teams in football to one on the brink of a championship. Of course, Bengals fans felt the same way about their team, and it appeared that 1987 would provide another long, entertaining race between the two Ohio teams for the division crown.

It would prove to be a bizarre season for all of pro football, a year defined by a month-long players strike that cancelled one week of games and saw three more weeks of "replacement" football when nonunion players were brought in to put on the uniforms and provide fractional talent. But before the strike put a sinkhole in the NFL season, Sam Wyche took a flamethrower to the Bengals' campaign.

Things started promisingly when Cincinnati went on the road in the opener and defeated an Indianapolis team that wound up winning the AFC East. Even better, in a Super Bowl XVI rematch with San Francisco at Riverfront the following week, the Bengals surged to a 20–7 halftime lead and had victory in their back pocket, holding a 26–20 lead and the ball with six seconds remaining. As close to guaranteed victory as a team could get in that situation, Wyche orchestrated a destructive Rube Goldberg strategy that, for some, defined his entire tenure in Cincinnati.

Facing fourth down from his own 30, Wyche opted not to take the risk of a blocked punt or an intentional safety. He sent his offense back onto the field with a play intended to chew up all of the remaining time. Instead, the Bengals' usually sterling offensive line melted like freshly drawn butter, and the 49ers instantly pinned James Brooks for a five-yard loss with two seconds left. It was a miserable play that gave San Francisco the ball back, but the 49ers still needed to go twenty-five yards in one play against a defense that had frustrated them all afternoon. The Bengals, despite the brain fart, were still in good shape.

In a mini-Hail Mary formation, the 49ers lined up three receivers on the left side and just one to the right. Common sense suggested quarterback Joe Montana would lob a pass up for grabs to his left and hope for the best. However, the lone receiver on the right wasn't just any pass catcher, but perhaps the best ever: Jerry Rice. He may have been in just his second season, but Bill Walsh—who, remember, could have been doing all of this *for* the Bengals instead of against them—knew what he had in Rice. The Bengals, in putting rookie cornerback Eric Thomas— who'd already surrendered a pair of touchdown passes on the day—in single coverage on Rice, did not.

Montana, not quite believing what he was seeing, dropped back and launched a pass for Rice, who'd turned Thomas inside out in the end zone and simply leaped up unimpeded and caught the ball for a touchdown with no time remaining. Moments later, the extra point gave the 49ers a 27–26 victory delivered in a fashion that may have justified firing Wyche on the spot. Shortly after the game, a phalanx of angry fans gathered in the parking lot and began chanting, "We want Sam!" And not in a rock-star kind of way. Firing him, or even extraditing him over to the fans, probably wouldn't have done any good, since the crushing defeat set the tone for the remainder of the Bengals season.

Instead of their first 2–0 start in six years, the Bengals were 1–1 heading into the strike. And after their replacement team split its first two games, it headed into the final week of scab football with the most bizarre Browns-Bengals game ever.

Even before the game started, Paul Brown was angry. Technically, the strike had ended the previous Thursday, when the players agreed to return to work. But since they hadn't done so before the league's pre-determined deadline of Wednesday, the players couldn't play in that Sunday's game. Sticking to its guns, the NFL opted to ride through one more week of replacement players, which, Paul Brown was quick to point out, gave the Browns a decided advantage as they arrived in Cincinnati. Nine regulars at key positions for the Browns had crossed the picket line, most notably backup quarterback Gary Danielson and wideout Brian Brennan. In union terms, the Bengals had stood together admirably, with only two players crossing the picket line to play during the strike. However, that unity proved damaging on the field in the final strike game as Danielson and Brennan nearly defeated the overmatched Cincinnati replacement defense by themselves. Brennan caught ten passes for 139 yards and Danielson threw four touchdown passes as the Browns outgained Cincinnati 410 total yards to ninety-five in a 34–0 rout.

For as happy as Paul Brown was to get his regulars back, the real frustration of the season began when things were back to normal. They blew double-digit fourth-quarter leads in their first two games back to lose to Pittsburgh and then Houston. A few weeks later, after committing five turnovers in a blowout loss to the Steelers at Riverfront, the Bengals dropped to 0–6 at home on the year.

The following week in the Meadowlands, they found yet another way to lose. Tied with the Jets, the Bengals were poised to win with a forty-six-yard field goal attempt with less than two minutes to play. Instead, New York blocked the kick and returned it sixty-seven yards for the game-winning touchdown. It was perhaps the defining moment of the Bengals' woeful season. Fittingly, after an ugly overtime win over a miserable Kansas City team to snap the string, the Bengals closed out the home schedule by blowing a 24–3 lead and allowing the New Orleans Saints to score thirty-eight unanswered points to close out the game. "My insides," Wyche confessed at one point, "are slowly eroding."

Even worse for Paul Brown, the week before, the Bengals had trekked to Cleveland and were throttled by the Browns, who once again were cruising toward the playoffs. With Kosar now unquestionably one of the league's finest quarterbacks and Lindy Infante pulling the strings on a well-balanced offense, the Browns endured a couple narrow losses to take control of the AFC Central and clinched it the day after Christmas with a gritty win over Pittsburgh that wrapped up a 10–5 regular season. Once again, the Browns went into the playoffs on a roll and efficiently wiped out Indianapolis in the divisional round, setting up the rematch with Denver they'd waited a year for.

The rematch, it turned out, may have been a better game than the original. This time, from sunshiny Mile High Stadium in Denver, the Browns imploded in the early going, digging a 21–3 halftime hole, then permitting an eighty-yard touchdown pass to make it 28–10 early in the third period. Then Kosar and the offense caught fire, putting together three straight touchdown drives to tie the contest at thirty-one with just over ten minutes remaining. Denver surged back ahead, 38–31, with four minutes left, then Kosar and the Browns got the ball back in what appeared would be their version of Elway's Drive from the year before. The Browns marched from their own 24 to the Denver 8 with just over a minute to play. A handoff to Earnest Byner—who'd played the game of his life—caught the Broncos on their heels, and Byner dashed inside the five. For just a moment, he appeared to tumble across the goal line for the game-tying touchdown. But he'd been stripped of the football at the two-yard line and the Broncos recovered, providing another soul-crushing defeat that would be memorialized in capital letters: The Fumble.

There was no reason to expect the Browns not to pick up where they'd left off in 1988. Led by Kosar, their core group of talent was returning, and Schottenheimer and his staff had built a formidable system that was poised to contend for years to come. But there was one change that would haunt the Browns—the same way it had haunted the Bengals five years earlier. Lindy Infante's success in turning the one-dimensional Cleveland offense into one of the best in the league hadn't gone unnoticed, and it came as no surprise when the Green Bay Packers offered him the head coaching position vacated by Forrest Gregg after the 1987 season. They were big shoes to fill, and while the Browns hadn't accelerated their own problems by forcing him out the door the way Paul Brown had, they committed the cardinal sin of not replacing him. Wanting to maintain the system Infante had built rather than bringing in a new coordinator and installing a new system, Schottenheimer took on the play-calling duties himself. After leading the Browns to three consecutive division titles and within a breath of the last two Super Bowls, Schottenheimer had enough clout that Modell went along.

The opposite power shift took place down Interstate 71. Everyone in the Western Hemisphere expected Sam Wyche to be fired after a disastrous season in which many of his colorful quirks as a head coach seemed to turn against him. Few, if any, NFL owners would have stuck with Wyche. Even before 1987, he hadn't made much of a positive impression. Nevertheless, Paul Brown, to his credit, decided to stick with Wyche—but only, he insisted, if Wyche reined in some of the nonsense and adopted a more traditional, by-the-book approach to coaching. He regulated Wyche's diet and sleep schedule and ensured that his coaching staff got home at a reasonable hour each night rather than burning the midnight oil in perpetuity. Like Forrest Gregg's decision to stick with Ken Anderson as his starting quarterback early in the 1981 season, Brown's choice to keep Wyche wound up being one of the great decisions in franchise history.

An apparently unremarkable game with the Phoenix Cardinals in Week One may have actually been the most important of the year. In a contest that mirrored the handful of blown opportunities and fourth-quarter meltdowns of the year before, the Bengals rallied from behind to surge ahead in the final minutes, then stopped the Cardinals when they had a chance to send the game to overtime. Just like that, the demons of 1987 were gone, and the Bengals were once again a very talented team playing with confidence.

They came from behind in the fourth quarter on the road to win the next two games, and Boomer Esiason had suddenly become the hottest quarterback in pro football, throwing nine touchdown passes in three weeks as the Bengals stood at 3–0 for the first time in thirteen years. But they couldn't really consider themselves legitimate until they took down their intrastate rivals. And right on cue, they came marching into Riverfront. Or what was left of them, anyway.

A season that had begun with so much promise and expectation—including Bernie Kosar plastered on *Sports Illustrated*'s pro football preview issue with a Super Bowl prediction for the Browns on the pages within—hit immediate turbulence. One quarter into the season, Kosar injured his elbow and was lost for six weeks—one of five injuries to starters the Browns suffered on opening day. Things got even worse in Week Two when backup quarterback Gary Danielson's season—and career—ended with a broken ankle. The Browns limped into their Week Four showdown with the Bengals with third-stringer Mike Pagel at the helm of a wheezing offense that hadn't scored a touchdown until its third game. The struggles continued at Riverfront when Kevin Mack fumbled on the game's fourth play and the Bengals scooped it up and returned it for a tone-setting touchdown. The overmatched Browns hung in, but the Bengals were simply too much. Instead of relying on Esiason and the much-ballyhooed passing attack, Cincinnati ground the Browns down with a dominating running game spearheaded by rookie Ickey Woods, who scored a pair of his fifteen touchdowns for the season. Now with a two-game lead over the Browns atop the AFC Central, it appeared as though there had been a power shift within the division.

With the win over the Browns, the Bengals were officially for real. But while Esiason and his cadre of talented receivers were still potent, the true strength of the Cincinnati offense was its running game. With versatile James Brooks as reliable as ever, Woods emerged as a star. The powerful fullback even cemented his legacy with a modified step-ball-change dance move he performed after each touchdown he scored, quickly named the "Ickey Shuffle." With the offense afire, they rolled up nearly 500 yards in a blowout win over the Raiders, then pounded the Jets and Oilers at Riverfront, where the hard-luck narrative of 1987 had taken a 180-degree turn. For the first time in its history, their cookie-cutter stadium had a personality. It was now referred to as "The Jungle," partially as a tie-in with the team's tiger motif, but more as an homage to the Guns N' Roses metal song "Welcome to the Jungle," which was rocketing up the charts in the fall of 1988. Suddenly unbeatable at home, the Bengals took an NFL-best 7-1 record into Halloween weekend for the most anticipated game of the year.

As the Bengals soared, the Browns had righted their ship, even after going to their fourth option at quarterback in thirty-eight-year-old Don Strock, hauled in off a Miami golf course to direct the Browns to a critical win over Philadelphia in Week Seven. Kosar returned the following week and threw three touchdown passes in a win at Phoenix that pulled them to 5-3. Next, they'd host the upstart Bengals, with revenge—and survival—the primary focus.

It was perhaps the high point in the history of the rivalry. The eyes of the football world were focused on Cleveland as the two title contenders clashed beneath a bright autumn sun on the final Sunday of October. Unlike the first meeting, the Browns held Cincinnati's running game in check and stymied Esiason, not allowing the league's top offense to score a touchdown. The game turned on a pair of huge plays by Cleveland's special teams. First was an eighty-four-yard kickoff return by utility running back Herman Fontenot to set up a touchdown after the Bengals had taken an early lead. Then, midway through the third quarter, the Browns took command when cornerback Frank Minnifield blocked a Cincinnati punt that Fontenot recovered and rolled into the end zone for a touchdown to put Cleveland up, 20–10. The Browns hung on for a seven-point win that pulled them within a game of the Bengals. With Kosar now healthy, it felt as though the Browns' experience might overcome the Bengals' verve.

But the issues that had haunted the Browns early in the year came back around in the final weeks. The offense under Schottenheimer's play calling remained erratic, and the team seemed prone to crippling mistakes. When Kosar went down again, this time to a knee injury in the penultimate game, it appeared the 9–6 Browns' playoff hopes were dashed. And indeed, forced to turn back to Don Strock for the finale against Houston with a wild-card spot on the line, the Browns coughed up four turnovers in the first half and fell behind, 23–7. But with snow blanketing the field, Strock turned in the performance of his life, leading the Browns back to a 28–23 win that secured a fourth straight playoff berth.

But for the first time in that string, they didn't capture the division title. The Bengals, bouncing back from the loss in Cleveland, remained ahead of both the Browns and Oilers in the final weeks, securing the AFC Central crown in dramatic fashion in Week Sixteen.

Despite a lackluster Saturday-afternoon performance at Riverfront against the going-nowhere Washington Redskins, the Bengals rallied from behind to tie the contest in the fourth quarter. They then dodged a massive bullet in the final seconds when the Redskins' reliable kicker Chip Lohmiller missed a chip-shot twenty-nine-yard field goal with eleven seconds left that would have won the game. The teams tumbled into overtime, where the Bengals won with their own chip-shot field goal, completing a clean eight-game sweep of the home schedule at Riverfront and a 12–4 record. Better still, when Buffalo lost to underdog Indianapolis the following day, the Bengals secured home-field advantage throughout the AFC playoffs.

Excluding the 1982 expanded postseason, it marked the first—and only—time the Browns and Bengals had both made the playoffs in the same year. And fittingly, each team's postseason experience mirrored its regular season.

In a quirk of coincidence, six days after the Browns defeated Houston in Cleveland to secure a playoff spot, the same two teams met on the same field in the AFC Wild Card Game on Christmas Eve. After a season defined by injury and frustration, the Browns had their share of both in the rematch. Don Strock—the hero the week before—injured his wrist on the first play of the second quarter, marking the fifth time in 1988 the Browns lost a quarterback to an injury. Mike Pagel, activated two days earlier after missing the previous two months with a shoulder injury, was thrust into the huddle and guided the Browns to a 16–14 lead late in the third quarter.

But as had been the case in the Browns' previous three trips to the playoffs, their defense wilted when it was needed most. Houston scored ten straight points to take a two-score lead and then held off the Browns, who pulled within a single point with a last-gasp touchdown in the final minute, for a 24–23 win. The Browns' season of massive expectations had ended in massive disappointment, and as the old ballpark on Lake Erie emptied that Christmas Eve, everyone knew there would be repercussions.

The Bengals, meanwhile, faced with lofty expectations as the conference's top seed, rose to the occasion. On New Year's Eve, they took care of business against Seattle, dominating the line of scrimmage and rolling up better than 250 rushing yards—126 from Ickey Woods—as they built a 21–0 halftime lead. They then held off the Seahawks— limited to just eighteen yards on the ground—and caught a huge break with six minutes to go. With its second touchdown, Seattle had an opportunity to pull within a single score. But the haunted goalposts at the south end of Riverfront emerged as a factor once again. The Seahawks missed the extra point, keeping the Bengals' margin at two scores and changing the complexion of the final minutes. Just like in Times Square a few hours later, the Cincinnati faithful counted down the final seconds as the Bengals moved to within one win of the Super Bowl.

Their final hurdle before reaching football's grand showcase would be the Buffalo Bills, who'd wilted down the stretch after an 11–1 start, costing them home field for the AFC Championship. Really, they'd never recovered after a 35–21 pounding the Bengals had delivered at Riverfront in Week Thirteen. Hoping to spike some of Cincinnati's momentum, the Bills tried a little gamesmanship leading up to the rematch. Complaining that the Bengals' no-huddle offense should be outlawed, the Bills successfully got the NFL to intervene. Less than two hours before kickoff, the Bengals were informed by the league they would be penalized if they attempted to use the no-huddle offense simply to draw a penalty. The league also landed another symbolic blow when it announced that Ickey Woods's now-famous "Shuffle" was considered an excessive celebration and wouldn't be allowed on the field.

For all the controversy, the Bengals weren't affected. In a game that played out very similarly to the original meeting, Cincinnati built an early lead and once again dominated time of possession with a strong running game. Woods again topped the 100-yard mark and scored a pair of touchdowns—sprinting to the sideline to perform the Shuffle each time—as the Bengals cruised to a 21–10 victory. It completed a perfect ten-game sweep of each contest played at Riverfront Stadium that season and one of the most incredible one-season turnarounds in NFL history. After a seven-year absence, the Bengals were headed back to the Super Bowl.

Waiting for them once again, almost poetically, were Bill Walsh and the San Francisco 49ers. Adding even more emotional weight, the contest would match Walsh with his former comrade Wyche, who had been hired for his first NFL coaching job by Walsh exactly ten years before.

With subplots already swirling, twenty-four hours before the game, the Bengals were confronted by a scandal. Running back Stanley Wilson—who had already scored three touchdowns in the postseason—was found in his hotel room high on cocaine. Since it marked Wilson's third violation of the NFL's drug policy, he was suspended for the game, and then banned from the league for life. The Bengals, like many NFL teams, had been rocked by drug use throughout the 1980s. But this incident struck an emotional and strategic blow to the team just hours before its biggest game.

Unlike their first Super Bowl showdown in Pontiac, this one was a nail-biter that went down to the wire—arguably the greatest Super

Bowl played up to that point. But for all the drama that would ensue in Miami that afternoon, many Bengals fans' first memory of the contest is of Tim Krumrie. Attempting to make a tackle early in the contest, their All-Pro defensive lineman caught his cleat in the turf and his leg twisted awkwardly, then snapped almost completely in half. The slow-motion replays were horrific enough to be almost unwatchable. Krumrie was obviously lost for the game, and Cincinnati was dealt another huge emotional blow. But the Bengals would endure.

In a surprisingly low-scoring game defined by defense, each team could manage just a field goal in the first half, but things ratcheted up in the second. A ninety-three-yard kickoff return for a touchdown by Cincinnati's Stanford Jennings gave the Bengals a 13–6 lead late in the third quarter, but the 49ers responded moments later with a touchdown by Jerry Rice—who was turning in one of the greatest performances in Super Bowl history.

Still, with the clock ticking down under five minutes, the Bengals took possession and slowly marched into San Francisco territory. A Jim Breech field goal with 3:44 to play put Cincinnati ahead, 16–13, and Paul Brown could taste his first championship in thirty-three years—particularly when a penalty on the ensuing kickoff pinned the 49ers back at their own eight-yard line. Eerily similar to what John Elway had done to the Browns two years before, Joe Montana drove his offense ninety-two yards, completing eight of nine passes along the way. The last was a ten-yard touchdown toss to wide receiver John Taylor, providing the winning points with thirty-four seconds left. It marked the 49ers' third title in eight seasons under Walsh—who retired a few days later—and was as close as any team had come to winning a Super Bowl without actually winning it. Once again, Bengals fans couldn't help but wonder: if only they'd played against any other team, against any other coach . . .

For all the heartbreak, it appeared as though the Bengals would have a good chance to get back to the Super Bowl. Now it was they who would have to shoulder the load of being a near-miss bridesmaid and champion-in-waiting, while the Browns would have to manage internal strife.

Understandably, Art Modell promised changes after the high promise of 1988 had gone awry. In the days after the season ended, he laid out a handful of demands to Marty Schottenheimer, including hiring an offensive coordinator and replacing a handful of assistant coaches. Schottenheimer, perhaps sensing that by no longer having control of his staff he was being set up to fail, refused, then resigned.

It was stunning news. For all his flaws, Schottenheimer had been the Browns' most successful head coach in the previous two decades, and, while 1988 had been defined by some poor decisions, in some ways it was his best coaching job. Now, in a blink, he was gone, and for the first time in eleven years, Art Modell needed to go shopping for a head coach.

He settled on longtime assistant Bud Carson, credited as the architect of Pittsburgh's Steel Curtain defense in the 1970s and the New York Sack Exchange while with the Jets in the '80s. Carson would, so the story went, take the Cleveland defense to the next level and bring an intensity that was notably absent when the chips were down in each heart-wrenching playoff loss under Schottenheimer.

It sounded great. And maybe, under ideal circumstances, could have worked. But behind the scenes, Modell was taking back much of the power that Schottenheimer had absorbed. Which may have been understandable, but Modell kept going, even dictating who many of Carson's assistants would be and taking much of the player personnel decision making out of his new coach's hands. It was abundantly clear that the team was Modell's, reflected by an uncharacteristic wheeling/dealing draft day that saw the Browns trade away proven commodities to land some potentially explosive playmakers like Texas running back Eric Metcalf. Little by little, the core of Schottenheimer's empire was whittled away, from nose tackle and hometown hero Bob Golic to running back Earnest Byner, whom the former coach had often called the heart of the team. Add to that the loss of Kevin Mack for much of the next year after he was arrested for possession of cocaine, and the Browns looked like an entirely different team by the time the 1989 season began.

But right out of the gate, it looked brilliant. In Carson's first game, the Browns annihilated Pittsburgh, 51–0, forcing eight turnovers and limiting the Steelers to a franchise-low fifty-three total yards. It was perhaps the greatest defensive performance in Cleveland history and made Art Modell look like a genius. Things kept rolling with another victory the following week, and the Browns were 2–0 for the first time in ten years. They'd face their first real test in Week Three with a trip to Cincinnati for a Monday-night showdown with the defending AFC champs.

Like their meeting in Cleveland eleven months earlier, it was one of the most anticipated chapters in the history of the rivalry. Both teams were coming off playoff seasons, and both expected more. After a narrow loss in Chicago to open the season, the Bengals pounded Pittsburgh at Riverfront in Week Two. But Ickey Woods—the rookie sensation from the year before—suffered a serious knee injury that ended his season and altered the course of what appeared would be a promising career. He would see limited action each of the next two years but would never again resemble the powerful downfield runner he'd been in 1988.

The 1970s conspiracy feel returned prior to kickoff when Wyche claimed to have caught the Browns a) trying to secretly videotape the Bengals' coaching staff's communications, and b) installing hidden microphones in their players' shoulder pads to record the Bengals' terminology. The Browns denied both charges, explaining that the equipment was part of a segment for a local television station that Wyche knew about. But Wyche—who'd accused the Seattle Seahawks of a similar type of chicanery four years before—would persist with the accusation for years.

With a national audience (and maybe the Browns' listening devices) tuned in, the teams put on an intense display. Even with Woods out, Cincinnati controlled the line of scrimmage, rushing for 187 yards on the night. Most of the action occurred in the second quarter, when the teams combined for four touchdowns, including a had-to-see-it-to-believe-it touchdown reception by Eric Metcalf in which the rookie somehow jumped and danced around a pair of Cincinnati tacklers coming at him from opposite directions and scooted into the end zone. Only after viewing slow-motion replays could one properly appreciate Metcalf's athleticism.

The game was tied at fourteen at the half, but the Bengals surged back ahead on an Esiason touchdown toss in the third quarter. With the Cleveland offense sputtering, the lead remained secure until the final minute, when the Browns drove inside the Cincinnati 10. The Cincinnati defense held strong and a fourth-down pass fell incomplete, locking up the Bengals' twelfth straight victory at Riverfront Stadium.

Both teams continued their upward trajectory over the next few weeks before each suffered a sudden bout with schizophrenia in mid-October. A mediocre Miami team beat the Browns in overtime one week, then went to Cincinnati the next and snapped the Bengals' Riverfront winning streak. A second straight home loss to a noncontender the following week dropped the Bengals to 4–3 and signified some serious red flags. Their doldrums carried into November, where a blowout loss to the Raiders in Los Angeles and a heartbreaking Monday-night defeat in Houston dropped the defending AFC champions to 5–5.

Following a seven-turnover debacle in a home loss to Pittsburgh, the Browns also stood at the .500 mark but found their footing and charged to four straight wins and a two-game lead over the Bengals. Now toiling primarily with Houston for first place in the AFC Central, the Browns appeared to have a clear path to the playoffs. Then Marty Schottenheimer came back to town, this time as the head coach of the Kansas City Chiefs, and rolled a grenade into the Cleveland tent. A long, sloppy defensive slugfest ended in a 10–10 stalemate. The Browns, battered and exhausted after five bruising quarters, had just three days to recover before playing on Thanksgiving Day. Not surprisingly, they were lethargic and impotent and outplayed by a miserable Detroit team in a 13–10 defeat.

Still, they held sole possession of first place and could stay on track by doling out some payback against the staggering Bengals in Week Thirteen. On a brutally cold Sunday in Cleveland, the Bengals landed a haymaker with a stunning 21–0 triumph—their largest margin of victory in Cleveland in thirteen years and the first time the Browns had been shut out at home since 1977. The following Sunday, the Browns lost again—this time blowing a ten-point second-half lead in Indianapolis, along with multiple chances to put the game away in the final minutes. An interception return for a Colts touchdown ended the contest in sudden-death overtime, and the Browns' winless streak had stretched to four games.

But the Browns' struggles weren't the primary topic of conversation in Cleveland—or anywhere in Ohio—the following week.

Just hours before the Browns squandered a potential victory in Indiana, the Bengals suffered their own inexplicable defeat that crippled their playoff chances. But while much of Cincinnati's 24–17 home loss to Seattle is forgotten, one moment is forever frozen in time.

As Seattle mounted a drive, fans at Riverfront began tossing snow-balls at the Seahawks from the stands. It was strikingly similar to an incident in Cleveland in October, when a barrage of items—with batteries now joining the usual fare of dog biscuits—was hurled at the Denver Broncos from the Dawg Pound, causing the officials to move the action to the other end of the field. Wyche, already a vocal critic of the shenanigans of the Pound and what he felt were lackluster efforts by the Browns organization to resolve the problem over the years, swore to pull his team off the field if anything like it ever happened when the Bengals were in town. Now the same thing was happening on his home field, and he wouldn't stand for it.

Wyche grabbed a handheld microphone from a team employee on the sideline and made a stirring announcement: "Will the next person who sees anybody throw anything point them out and get them out of here?" he snarled.

He could have left it there. It was already an unorthodox and dramatic moment that grabbed everyone's attention and made the point. But he just couldn't help himself.

As a coda, he added with great vigor, "You don't live in Cleveland, you live in Cincinnati!"

The crowd roared with satisfaction and pride, then proceeded to watch the Bengals piss away another winnable game.

Still, almost as if by design, all anyone could talk about afterward was Wyche's impromptu public service announcement. While most Cincinnatians saw it as a rousing moment, the hometown paper couldn't get behind the coach. "This remark brought a big cheer, but it was way beyond the bounds of good taste," Tim Sullivan wrote in the *Enquirer*. "He had gone too far, again, and there was no one to stop him." Clevelanders, of course, took issue with the comment. But the *Plain Dealer* encouraged them not to blame Cincinnati or its fans. As one columnist wrote, "It's not their fault their football squad is in the hands of an unstable towel-snapper who leads the league in whining and always seems to be on the verge of a nervous breakdown when his team goes in the tank."

Not doing anything to change that opinion, Wyche followed up his improv act by banning reporters from the locker room after the game—a first in franchise history—and earned a $3,000 fine for violating league policy.

But still, rarely had the rivalry reached such a level of intensity—and the teams weren't even on the same field. In many ways, it seemed to mirror the long, offbeat history the two teams had shared together. Perhaps if the teams still had one more meeting that season after Wyche's manifesto, the rivalry could have truly taken off and become the stuff of legend. But instead, the season came to its dramatic conclusion without a head-to-head confrontation. (There was something of a comical climax to the story the following summer, when Wyche good-naturedly agreed to sit in a dunking booth in downtown Cleveland, where fans paid for a shot to drop him into a tank of water, with proceeds going to charity.)

The Browns got their act together to win back-to-back dramatic games. First was a frosty overtime affair with Minnesota decided by a touchdown on a fake field goal. Then came a Saturday-night shootout in Houston in which the Browns blew a seventeen-point lead before capturing the division title when embattled Kevin Mack plowed into the end zone for the game-winning—and season-saving—touchdown in the final minute.

Sam Wyche and the Bengals, meanwhile, found another gear in the next-to-last week. Needing to win both of their final games and then get some help to sneak into the playoffs, the Bengals had plenty of motivation going into their rematch with first-place Houston. And they got off to a great start, scoring three touchdowns in the first quarter and cruising to a 31–0 halftime lead. But with the bumbling Oilers already turning their attention to the next week's showdown with the Browns, the Bengals hit the gas.

Leaving his starters in and not changing the attack mentality, Wyche swelled the lead to 45–0. Then, after an onside kick—yes indeed, an onside kick—it extended to 52–0 before the third quarter was over. Best yet, with time running out and no reason in the world to do it, Wyche called time-out and sent his field-goal unit onto the field to kick a short field goal to push the Bengals up over sixty points. Wyche later said he wished there had been a fifth quarter, so the Bengals could have taken a shot at triple digits.

The final was 61–7—the largest margin of victory in franchise history and the most points the Bengals had scored in a game since 1972. Some joked that Wyche may have been hoping to score enough points to win two games at once. In a way, that's exactly what he was trying to do.

It was a doubly calculated move. Wyche, like many in the NFL, couldn't stand Houston head coach Jerry Glanville and his attitude-challenged Oilers, so piling it on to send a message was mostly vengeful. But it also had its strategic merits. For the fourth time in 1989, the Bengals' opponent one week would be the Browns' opponent the next. Cincinnati had won its game in the first three instances and in the last two had piled it on an overmatched opponent well after the outcome had been determined. On some level, Wyche was looking ahead to the following week—and by hanging a lopsided score on the Browns' next opponent, the Bengals were obliquely angering and motivating the beaten team to come out with something to prove the following game.

The strategy had worked. On all three occasions, the team blown out by the Bengals was decidedly sharper the next week against Cleveland, and twice the heavily favored Browns had been tripped up. With their destiny now not entirely in their control, the Bengals needed Houston to beat the Browns in the finale to give them a chance to leapfrog Cleveland for the final wild card spot.

It didn't quite work. With the Browns' dramatic victory, Houston was relegated to the wild card game, where it lost to underdog Pittsburgh on a last-second field goal. Days later, Glanville was fired—never having put his team back on the rails after the blowout in Cincinnati.

But the Bengals still had a chance to slip into the postseason. With a victory in Minnesota on Christmas night, they'd earn the second wild card spot and set up what would have been a truly intriguing rematch with the Oilers in Houston a week later. But the Vikings, also needing a win to clinch their division and earn a playoff spot, built a commanding halftime lead (aided by five Bengals turnovers on the night) and hung on for a 29–21 win that ended a bipolar Bengals season with an appropriate 8–8 record.

The Browns, nearly equally unpredictable, had managed a 9–6–1 mark and hosted Buffalo in a memorable divisional playoff game. The attack defense that Bud Carson had been hired to build to take the Browns over the hump Marty Schottenheimer could never surmount was shredded for 400 passing yards from Bills quarterback Jim Kelly. Only a dropped touchdown pass and a goal line interception in the final seconds enabled the Browns to escape with a 34–30 win. There was no such luck the following week.

Facing Denver for a trip to the Super Bowl for the third time in four years, this time the Browns were simply overmatched. The defense was carved up again, this time for nearly 500 total yards, as the Broncos cruised to a 37–21 victory and another Super Bowl beating—this one at the hands of San Francisco, which followed up its win over the Bengals the previous year to become the NFL's first repeat champion in ten years.

For both the Browns and the Bengals, 1989 was a canary in a mine shaft for what was to come. Both teams still had substantial talent, but major problems had begun to be exposed, and age and talent depletion had begun to slide the championship window of opportunity closed.

The Browns entered freefall first. All the defensive problems from the final games of 1989 resurfaced again in 1990, now combined with a shoddy offense. They lost three of their first four games, rebounded to notch a dramatic last-second victory over Denver on a Monday night, then lost eight in a row.

The season really entered disaster mode in another *Monday Night Football* appearance two weeks later, when the Bengals came to Cleveland. Cincinnati had shrugged off its 1989 struggles to once again begin the season 4–1. After Boomer Esiason threw for 490 yards in a Week Five overtime victory over the Los Angeles Rams, it appeared the Bengals were back up to their 1988 standard. They hit a speed bump with a blowout loss in Houston, as the Oilers avenged their massacre in Cincinnati the year before, and another with a Monday-night loss in Seattle— underscored by Wyche drawing attention away from a lackluster performance once again when he barred a female reporter from the locker room afterward. But they'd have a chance to reaffirm their status against the struggling Browns.

Cleveland hung close for a half, but the Bengals pulled away for seventeen unanswered second-half points in a 34–13 triumph that put them three full games ahead of the Browns and essentially forced their intrastate rivals to abandon any hopes of a turnaround in 1990. Sure enough, Bud Carson was fired two weeks later, and assistant Jim Shofner was given the unenviable task of finishing the season. He did, but only after losses of 58–14 to Houston and 35–0 to Pittsburgh clearly demonstrated how far the defending division champions had fallen.

Meanwhile, the Bengals staggered toward their second AFC Central crown in three years. Following the win in Cleveland, the erratic ups and downs of the previous season returned. Three losses in their next four games—two at home to teams with losing records—dropped the Bengals into a three-way race for first with equally unpredictable Houston and Pittsburgh. But a season sweep of the Steelers and a rousing victory over the Oilers in Week Sixteen put the Bengals in the pole position for the division title. All they needed was a win in the finale over (predictably) the Browns. For the tenth time, the Browns and Bengals squared off in a December showdown with one team on the brink of the playoffs and the other out to spoil the party.

Nobody expected it to be an entertaining game. Indeed, after the Bengals—sixteen-point favorites—jumped to a 14–0 lead, it appeared the Browns were on the brink of another lopsided defeat. But the 3–12 Browns, with absolutely nothing to play for, rallied. Backup quarterback Mike Pagel, filling in for battered Bernie Kosar, guided the Browns to a pair of touchdowns to tie the game going into the fourth quarter. Cincinnati surged back ahead on a short Esiason touchdown pass with ten minutes remaining, but the Browns mounted another rally. Only after a dropped fourth-down pass by the Browns and then an interception, both deep in Cincinnati territory in the final five minutes, was the game—and the division title—secured for the Bengals.

In some ways, it was a fitting game to be the last Browns-Bengals contest Paul Brown would ever witness. It encapsulated so much of the twenty-year history of the rivalry: one team steaming toward the playoffs, the other going nowhere. But against all logic, an entertaining contest emerged. It also closed out the golden era of the rivalry—the first and last period in which both teams were strong at the same time for an extended period.

While the Browns limped into the offseason to begin another

coaching search and roster overhaul, the Bengals embarked on what would be their last playoff experience for a decade and a half. They steamrolled past Houston in a Riverfront rematch, then jetted west for a divisional playoff encounter with the Raiders, which not only turned out to mark the end of an era for the Bengals, but for one of the legendary players in NFL history. Early in the third quarter, Raiders iconic running back Bo Jackson was tackled awkwardly after a long run and dislocated his hip. No one knew it at the time, but after lighting the professional sports world afire by dominating play in both the NFL and Major League Baseball, Jackson's football career ended on that play.

Even without Jackson for the remainder of the afternoon, the Raiders were able to handle equally injury-riddled Cincinnati, pulling away in the fourth quarter for a 20–10 victory in what turned out to be the final game the Bengals would play under the ownership of Paul Brown.

Seven months later, he was gone. And so would begin the long search for the souls of both the Browns and the Bengals—a sojourn that would reach its wayward crescendo in the second decade of the new century.

8

One and Done
2009–present

If the ups and downs of the Browns and Bengals of the late 1980s were represented by hit songs—whether "Bernie Bernie" or "Welcome to the Jungle"—more recently the year-by-year rhythms of both teams have been as solemn and predictable as a metronome. One team's modest (yet still frustrating) success based on rote consistency, the other's epic failures based on a complete lack of it.

While the Bengals enjoyed an unexpected renaissance in 2009, give the Browns credit for finding a way to get worse following what appeared to be a rock-bottom season—a trait they'd hone to perfection in the years to come. Bill Belichick disciple Eric Mangini—who'd been a *Devil Wears Prada*-type intern during Belichick's Cleveland regime in the mid-'90s—attempted to bring a grown-up sensibility to Romeo Crennel's discipline-challenged Camp Cupcake. (A reputation tragically underscored once again that offseason when wide receiver Donte Stallworth, with a blood alcohol level nearly twice the legal limit, ran over and killed a pedestrian with his car.)

But now the pendulum had swung too far the other way. Mangini—who'd earned the nickname "Mangenius" for his success as an assistant and then during a short stint as head coach of the Jets—was accused of orchestrating overly intense and long practices that beat up and beat down his own players. And the apparent abuse wasn't just physical. Players were cut for talking back to coaches and not running at full speed during punitive postpractice laps. The comical breaking point may have been when a player was fined $1,700 for taking a $3 bottle of water from a hotel without paying for it. Braylon Edwards was traded away after allegedly punching a friend of Cavaliers star LeBron James at a nightclub, and rumors swirled of an anarchic *Mortal Kombat* scene at halftime of a game in Chicago that saw Browns players fighting with other players, players fighting with coaches, and even coaches fighting with coaches.

The result was a 1–11 start that had rumors swirling about the Mangenius not being brought back for a second year. A puzzling (and deceiving) four-game winning streak to close out the schedule likely saved Mangini's job and saw the Browns pulling a page from the Bengals' 1990s book of late-season mirages. To his credit, after the turmoil, owner Randy Lerner wisely decided that the team needed a veteran football voice to bring stability to a franchise gone bananas. Unfortunately, even that wound up making things worse.

The Browns quickly bumbled away their sudden momentum by losing five of six to start 2010. But they just as inexplicably found their mojo again, picking up back-to-back incomprehensible blowout victories over the defending Super Bowl-champion New Orleans Saints and the perennially dominant New England Patriots. Fueled by the out-of-nowhere urban legend mythos and bulging biceps of battering-ram running back Peyton Hillis, they clawed to the cusp of playoff contention before once again closing the season on a four-game streak—this time all losses. And while the 2009 streak saved Mangini's job, the 2010 streak lost it.

Which was just as well, really, because Mangini hadn't been embraced by the Browns' new president—Randy Lerner's mustachioed Rock of Gibraltar. Former Green Bay Packers and Seattle Seahawks Head Coach Mike Holmgren, looking to graduate to the next level of football imperialism after serving as a general manager, brashly strode into Cleveland and fully expected to turn the Browns around in about forty-five minutes.

"Don't come to me for extra tickets for a playoff game," Holmgren arrogantly snapped at reporters at a press conference during a six-game losing streak in 2011. With a ludicrous five-year, $40 million contract in his back pocket, he brought in a new general manager (the team's third in three years) and began yet another overhaul of the roster. In retrospect years later, Holmgren admitted he probably should have just stepped in and coached the team, but that Lerner didn't want him to. So he inexplicably stuck with Mangini, who wasn't his guy, for one more uncomfortable season (5–11), then brought in woefully in-over-his-head (and, not for nothing, nephew of an old friend of Holmgren's) Pat Shurmur for two even more uncomfortable seasons (4–12 and 5–11).

Meanwhile, Peyton Hillis's lunch-break brush with fame came to an abrupt halt. After rushing for 1,100 yards in 2010, he was an afterthought candidate in EA Sports' first-ever online fan vote to determine who would appear on the next edition of the wildly popular Madden video game. With a groundswell of ensorcelled Browns fans voting for what they were convinced was the franchise's next Jim Brown, Hillis won—beating out a handful of Canton-bound All-Pros along the way—and appeared on the cover of Madden 12 the following summer.

Shortly after the game hit the shelves, Hillis's career headed for the clearance rack. A long-alluded long-term contract with the Browns never evolved, and the lovefest began to sour when he sat out an early season game with strep throat. It didn't quite check out with Hillis's blue-collar, tough-guy personality and playing style, and he later admitted he skipped the game on the advice of his agent. It looked and sounded like a ham-fisted negotiation ploy. A hamstring injury muddled the rest of his season, and the Browns didn't even bother making an offer to Hillis when he became a free agent that winter. He played parts of three more years with the Chiefs and Giants but was never anywhere close to the type of player he was for that one golden season in Cleveland. Those who believe in curses were convinced Hillis was the casualty of the bad juju from a perceived Madden cover jinx. Realistic Browns fans knew Hillis was doomed long before he became football's Lara Croft.

One of Hillis's first great moments in emerging as Cleveland's latest great orange hope was a 100-yard performance in an October victory over Cincinnati that sent the Bengals spiraling into a ten-game losing streak—their worst since the woebegone mid-1990s. The Bengals dropped from 10–6 in 2009 to 4–12 in 2010, and once again, there were vociferous calls for Marvin Lewis's job.

Things got even worse a month after the season ended when Carson Palmer, the face of the franchise for seven years, threatened to retire if he wasn't traded, then backed it up by refusing to play for the Bengals and sitting out the first six weeks of the 2011 season. Mike Brown, after initially refusing to reward Palmer by trading him, finally gave in and shipped him off to the resurgent but desperate Oakland Raiders, who'd just lost starting quarterback Jason Campbell to a broken collarbone. Oakland coach and acting GM Hue Jackson (keep that name in mind, sports fans) shipped away first- and second-round draft picks to get Palmer, which the Bengals then used to land a pair of starters that would play key roles in the years to come.

At the time, Jackson called it "the greatest trade in football," which might actually have been true, but certainly not from the perspective of the team for which he worked. For starters, it seemed like a lot to give up to land a guy who wasn't even playing. It got even worse after Palmer arrived and the Raiders lost four of their last five games to finish 8–8, then fell to 4–12 the following year with Palmer as the full-time starter. Two months after acquiring Palmer, Hue Jackson was abruptly fired as Oakland's coach, partially because of the perception that he got schnookered in the trade. In a curious twist, he found safe haven by returning to Cincinnati (where he'd been the wide receivers coach during the original Lewis renaissance), this time as special teams coach. He would be promoted twice in the next three years, eventually becoming the Bengals' offensive coordinator—rehabilitating his career to the point where he'd once again get a chance to become a head coach who could lead a team to abject disappointment.

With Jackson back in the fold, and with the addition of the new players the Bengals had acquired with the draft picks Jackson himself had foolishly sent them, Marvin Lewis's second wind kicked in. It started the same year Palmer was traded. In what probably should have been another disastrous season, the 2011 Bengals rebounded to 9–7 behind rookie quarterback Andy Dalton and returned to the playoffs. It was another quick stay—a blowout wild-card loss to Houston—but marked the beginning of a streak that was both impressive and maddening.

For five straight years, the Bengals would reach the postseason, then lose their first game. Twice as a division champion, twice with home-field advantage, three times as a wild card, four times following a double-digit-win season. Each time, one and done.

They became the only team in NFL history to reach the postseason five straight years without picking up a playoff win. When you put it all together, it was a string of six first-round losses in seven years and a grand total of eight consecutive postseason defeats—which at the time matched the all-time NFL record.

A remarkable string that began, naturally, the year Paul Brown died.

***

In retrospect, the 2009 season served as a microcosm for the trends both the Bengals and Browns would establish in the years to come: frustratingly predictable constancy for one and drug-addict-level erraticism for the other.

Over the period that would follow, the Browns made massive front office changes seemingly by the hour. The Bengals, by the millennium.

A big part of Cincinnati's success in the second decade of the twenty-first century (regular season success, anyway) was consistency. Despite several near-coaching-death experiences, Marvin Lewis eventually became the second-longest tenured coach in the league (behind only Sith Lord Bill Belichick), keeping his system and much of his coaching staff in place for well over a decade. And of course, Mike Brown was still there to keep on keepin' on.

Really, you could argue that throughout the Bengals' "lost decade" that started in the 1990s, they were equally consistent in the front office. For years, Mike Brown basically ran the whole circus. And whatever marginal assistance he received came from people who had the same last name. At the turn of the century, five members of the Brown family earned salaries over $3 million from the Bengals. Further rankling fans was Brown paying himself a $1 million bonus each year for serving—quite badly—as the team's general manager. "He would rather run the Cincinnati Bengals into the ground," *Enquirer* columnist Tim Sullivan once wrote, "than let someone else steer."

The turning point was the arrival of Marvin Lewis. Partially it was because of the maturity he brought to the sideline and the locker room. But there was also the common sense he brought to longer-term decisions. Gradually, Mike Brown (and his blood-related subordinates) began to loosen the purse strings. After employing just one full-time scout for years, the Bengals finally staffed up to the level of four or five that many (if not most) NFL teams were at. They eschewed their annual tradition of being one of the last teams to sign its top draft pick. They upgraded their training facilities, which not long before had been defined by the stench of nearby Mill Creek, one of the most contaminated waterways in America. They stopped nickel-and-diming everybody and everything in sight—for example, charging their own players for breakfast at the stadium and taking their agents out to lunch at Wendy's during contract negotiations.

Mike Brown also began to loosen his comic book-villain grip on the franchise, or at least let the Bengals' inner circle grow larger than his own sportcoat. Lewis and his coaching staff began to play a larger role in personnel decisions, and it paid off in very visible ways. Quarterback Andy Dalton, for instance, wasn't Mike Brown's preference in the 2011 draft, but the Bengals drafted him anyway. Then they watched him lead the team to its five straight playoff appearances, a run that likely never would have materialized had Mike Brown still been the only one in the cockpit.

Nevertheless, the family-business mentality remained. Even back in the early days of the franchise, everybody knew Mike and Pete Brown were heavily involved with the operations, but nobody really understood exactly what their roles were. That element of the unknown persevered into the Bengals' renaissance, as the organizational structure of the front office remained mysterious. Mike Brown had become the Willy Wonka of the NFL: his factory spewed smoke out of its stacks, but nobody really knew what he was doing or how he was doing it.

Meanwhile, the Browns of the twenty-first century have essentially been doomed by the same thing that drove Paul Brown and the first rendition of the franchise out of Cleveland in the first place: clown-shoes ownership.

Things really went off the rails for the Browns before the rails had even been installed. In a bitter twist of irony lost to most fans in the anticipatory glow of the Browns' impending return to reality in 1999, the team's new owner turned out to be the same man who'd helped Art Modell orchestrate the original Browns' move to Baltimore in the first place. Billionaire investor Al Lerner—a minority owner of the Browns and a longtime friend of Modell—wound up essentially driving the getaway car. He introduced Modell to key people in Baltimore and helped his old friend seal the deal that ripped the team from Cleveland. Symbolically, the agreement to move the Browns to Baltimore was signed on one of Lerner's private jets.

Three years later, he owned the Browns. Seem weird?

But for the first few years of expansion, it seemed to be working out. Under Lerner's leadership, the Browns steadily improved each of their first four seasons back, even with a whoops-hit-the-brakes coaching change after Year Two. But midway through the 2002 season, Lerner died of brain cancer. His son Randy took over control of the franchise at the relatively youthful age of forty, and for the next decade, things were not great. *Aggressively* not great.

Not unlike Mike Brown trying to fill the shoes of his father, it became pretty clear pretty quickly that Randy Lerner wasn't cut out for the job. But whereas Mike Brown was labeled as a spendthrift, Randy Lerner fell into the less-populated "charitable-but-gullible" millionaire category. Fans saw him as simply disengaged, rarely appearing in Cleveland and often not involving himself in team operations. He left those duties to the men he hired to run the team—who were, almost unilaterally, terrible at their jobs.

Fans bristled even more when Randy Lerner bought the Aston Villa Premier League English soccer team in 2006, and it quickly became apparent that's where his heart—and interest—lay. But even that experience was an epic fail. Ten years later, he sold the team after losing $400 million and seeing it reach heretofore unseen levels of terrible. In 2011, *Forbes Magazine* ranked Randy Lerner as the fourth-worst NFL owner, and most felt that was gracious.

So when Jimmy Haslam arrived on the scene in 2012, he was seen as a white knight riding a fiery steed. Essentially pimped out by the NFL to Randy Lerner as a preapproved buyer, Haslam was a Tennessee billionaire whose father had founded Pilot Flying J, the largest operator of travel centers in North America. But just as troubling for Browns fans as Al Lerner's shady background with Art Modell, prior to buying the Browns, Haslam had been a minority owner of the Pittsburgh Steelers. Neither the Browns nor the NFL has ever quite understood that optics do matter.

Haslam strode into Cleveland with a reputation as a hands-on, no-nonsense businessman who wouldn't tolerate the incompetence Randy Lerner tended to ignore. Mike Holmgren, brought in to run the team so Lerner wouldn't have to, saw the writing on the wall and left town within days. Browns fans weren't so lucky. For it didn't take long to see Haslam's "hands on" modus operandi less as engaged than gropey.

His first order of business was to do something even Mike Brown or Randy Lerner never had the cojones to do, likely out of fear of what their respective fathers would think. Scoffing at sentimentality, Haslam promptly sold the naming rights of Cleveland Browns Stadium, forever removing the imprint of the team and its namesake and ensuring that for the first time in their seven decades of existence, the Browns would play in a corporate-sponsored ballpark. For a franchise that already appeared to be jinxed, this was the equivalent of breaking a mirror *while* walking under a ladder.

Next on Haslam's list—after not ruling out the possibility of ripping up the stadium grass in favor of artificial turf and putting a dome atop the stadium—was to shitcan the team's base uniform that had stood relatively consistent since Paul Brown had roamed the sidelines. After two years of planning, the new uniforms were unveiled in 2015—a mishmash of Reese's Pieces jersey-and-pants combinations that made the Browns look like the best-dressed high school team in the NFL. Immediately and universally hated by fans and players alike, within two years, discussions began about changing them once again—maybe this time, some whispered, with all-white helmets.

But these changes were just cosmetic. Truck Stop Jimmy Haslam was just getting warmed up.

First there was a little speed bump. Within six months of Haslam assuming ownership of the team, Flying J was caught defrauding customers out of millions of dollars in gas rebates. FBI agents raided Haslam's office like a Prohibition speakeasy, and there was a possibility that the Browns' new owner might be running the team from a jail cell—making Randy Lerner's Magic 8 Ball leadership seem like a golden age. Haslam managed to avoid prison, but his company paid roughly $150 million in penalties and restitution. Browns fans would soon know what that felt like.

In Haslam's first three seasons as owner, the Browns had three different head coaches and three different general managers—the last of whom, Ray Farmer, defined his short-lived career as GM by earning a four-game suspension and costing the team a quarter-million-dollar fine for texting Browns coaches during games in violation of league rules. But even in the aftermath of "TextGate," Farmer got to keep his job, which was a better deal than those who came before and after him. Each of Haslam's first two years of ownership ended with him firing his head coach and GM, something he'd do a third time after his fourth season, when Farmer and his scandalous cell phone were both inevitably let go. That day of reckoning brought the number of fired Browns head coaches since 1999 to seven, with a combined total of eighteen years remaining on their contracts—meaning the team had paid an estimated $56 million to seven lucky guys for the sole function of *not* coaching the Browns. Which might have been the best job in the history of jobs.

The first flaming wagon wheel came rolling into the campsite two games into Haslam's first full season as owner. With three months to go, the Browns essentially gave up on the season, trading away starting running back Trent Richardson seventeen months after making him the third overall pick in the draft. And when the 4–12 campaign was mercifully over, Haslam fired first-year coach Rob Chudzinski—whom he himself had hired less than a year earlier—to make it clear everything was Chudzinski's fault.

By the time websites and magazines began compiling their annual "worst sports owners" articles the following year, Jimmy Haslam had already done most of their work for them. For all intents and purposes, they simply inserted his name into Randy Lerner's spot. And he's been there ever since.

***

Whoever the Cleveland owner, whoever the general manager, whoever the coach, they all shared one mortifying legacy: an inability to settle on a starting quarterback.

For as disappointing as the Tim Couch era was, in retrospect, it was the good old days. Following four straight seasons of Couch being the no-doubt-about-it starting quarterback, the Browns began each of the next four years with a different quarterback starting the season—a gob-stoppingly amazing accomplishment that couldn't possibly be repeated . . . until they immediately did it again. After Charlie Frye's fifteen-minute tenure as the starter in 2007 snapped the string, the Browns began each of the next *five* seasons with a different quarterback. And finally, after Brandon Weeden (drafted in the first round at the sunset-years age of twenty-eight in 2012) spent a miserable two-year sentence in the Cleveland huddle, the Browns rebooted the position again each of the *next* four years.

In fact, when DeShone Kizer was named the quarterback to start the 2017 season, he became the Browns' twenty-seventh starting quarterback since their return in 1999. To be fair, a handful of the twenty-seven were backups and backups of backups forced into emergency/sacrificial coverage. But nearly half of them began a season taking over as the starter for someone else from the previous opening day. Thirteen times in fifteen seasons, the Browns trotted out a new starting quarterback to begin the year. (By contrast, over the same period, the Bengals had six different opening day starters and a grand total of nine starting quarterbacks.) All of this for a franchise that opened for business with Otto Graham leading it to ten championship games in ten years.

There were so many quarterbacks, it's easier to remember them by category than by name.

There were the Band-Aids—veterans picked up out of a desperate attempt to bring some semblance of dependability: Jeff Garcia, Trent Dilfer, Jake Delhomme, and Robert Griffin III.

There were the accidents—guys brought in as backups who, to the embarrassment of many, proved to be better (if only marginally) than the starters they were backing up: Kelly Holcomb, Derek Anderson, Seneca Wallace, Brian Hoyer, Jason Campbell, and Josh McCown.

There were the high draft picks—young promise and big-bonus money that never truly amounted to anything: Tim Couch, Brady Quinn, Colt McCoy, and Brandon Weeden.

And then there was Johnny Football.

It's difficult to imagine Paul Brown agreeing to even make eye contact with such a creature as Johnny Manziel. A runt-of-the-litter hashtag at Texas A&M, Manziel was seen by any true football mind as exactly what he was: all sizzle and no steak.

Talent (or lack thereof) aside, there were warning signs that he was more trouble than he was worth long before the Browns ever blighted their roster with his name. Two years before, at the age of nineteen, he was arrested for fighting and carrying a fake ID. The following summer, amid rumors he was thrown out of the prestigious Manning Passing Academy for partying, he was bounced from a University of Texas frat party, then triggered an NCAA investigation and half-game suspension for getting paid for autographs.

In addition to the scandals, there was an uncomfortable (and, many would argue, unjustified) arrogance about him that seemed to invite contempt, symbolized by his trademark "money" gesture of holding his hands above his head and rubbing his fingers together. But, in the overly drawn-out ramp-up to the draft, Manziel claimed that he was abandoning the more juvenile "Johnny Football" persona and dedicating himself to taking his craft more seriously. (Insert sitcom laugh track here.)

As the first round of the 2014 draft unfolded and team after team passed on Manziel like a rotten kumquat, he texted the Browns—who, as always, were looking for a new quarterback—and asked that they draft him so they could "wreck this league together." Following the advice of a homeless person he'd talked to outside a Cleveland restaurant earlier that day, Truck Stop Jimmy Haslam commanded his brain trust to abandon their draft strategy and take Manziel. Having no choice but to follow the order of a CEO gone wild, they did, and the more mature, more serious Manziel took the stage making his signature money fingers gesture. The horror show that everybody knew would be a horror show was up and running.

Before Manziel even put on a helmet, the Browns knew they'd made a mistake. The summer was filled with photographs of Manziel partying (one of him floating in a pool on an inflatable swan holding a bottle of champagne) and a video of him pretending a stack of cash was a cell phone (or perhaps genuinely not being able to tell which was which). His initial impact on the field took place in an exhibition game, when he gave the middle finger to the Washington Redskins bench. He endeared himself to the Cleveland fan base in November when his entourage beat up a fan who'd approached Manziel in an apartment building lobby. He made his first NFL start three weeks later—ironically, against the Cincinnati Bengals, who were no strangers to this type of character—and was miserable, throwing for a meager eighty yards and two interceptions in a 30–0 Bengals blowout. Two weeks after that, he missed a team walk-through and admitted he'd been out partying the night before. A month later, he checked into rehab, where he stayed for the next ten weeks.

Manziel's inspiring turnaround lasted almost six months. In October, he was questioned by police for driving dangerously following an alleged domestic dispute with his girlfriend. In the weeks to come, he was, in order:

a. Named the full-time starter for the rest of the season.
b. Caught on video partying on multiple occasions (once in disguise).
c. Promptly demoted to third string on the depth chart for his bizarre and distracting behavior.

The behavior would only get more bizarre and distracting from there. In January, police once again investigated another potential domestic dispute involving Manziel, whose girlfriend expressed concern about his well-being (and, presumably, hers). Later reports stated that Manziel had threatened to kill both her and himself, then hit her and dragged her by her hair into his car.

In the days to come, his father confessed he didn't think Manziel would live to see his twenty-fourth birthday. His agent dropped him as a client. And finally—inevitably—the Browns released him, just twenty-two months after pissing away a first-round draft choice on him. To the surprise of no one, no other teams offered Manziel a contract, and his wackadoodle NFL career ended with a grand total of two victories deliv-ered. It's possible Jimmy Haslam may have regretted taking draft advice from a hobo.

The real tragedy of the Manziel story, though, isn't what the Browns endured, but what they could have had. They'd passed up eventual All-Pro quarterbacks Teddy Bridgewater and Derek Carr in the draft to pick Manziel and eventually let Cleveland native Brian Hoyer walk in free agency after posting a 10–6 record as the Browns starting quarterback over two seasons.

Hoyer's unlikely and rapid rise from third string to starter could have been one of the great stories in recent Browns history, one that the fran-chise could have rallied a weary fan base around. With hometown kid Hoyer at the helm in the first half of Manziel's rookie season of 2014, the Browns surged to a 6–3 start and grabbed sole possession of first place in the AFC North after a stunning 24–3 Thursday-night blowout of the Bengals in Cincinnati the first week of November. But, of course, things soured, the Browns lost six of their final seven, and Manziel was cata-pulted into a lineup that he would poison throughout the following year as the Browns dropped from 7–9 to 3–13 in 2015. Meanwhile, Brian Hoyer led his new team, the Houston Texans, into the playoffs.

While letting go of a talented player they had under contract was a refreshing new flavor of incompetence, passing up eventual stars in the draft was nothing new for the Browns. Long before Johnny Football, it was a skill they'd honed and mastered, starting in 1999 when they went with Tim Couch over quarterback Donovan McNabb and running back Edgerrin James. The following year, they passed up eventual seven-time Pro Bowl linebacker Brian Urlacher and five-time Pro Bowl defensive end John Abraham to select injury-prone defensive lineman Court-ney Brown, whose unremarkable Cleveland career ended after missing thirty-three games over five seasons.

What would superstar running back LaDanian Tomlinson have looked like in orange and brown? Or dominant defensive end Richard Seymour? We'll never know, because the Browns preferred "Big Money" Gerard Warren, who endured four underachieving seasons on the defensive line. Similar story the next year, when they passed up safety Ed Reed and running backs Clinton Portis and Brian Westbrook for fellow running back William Green, whose most memorable achievement with the Browns was explaining to police that he'd fallen over backward onto a steak knife during a domestic dispute in 2003—a week after earning a four-game suspension for violating the league's drug policy.

Two years after that, the Browns went with tight end Kellen Winslow II but wouldn't see him play in extended action for two years. He broke his leg in an ill-advised onside kick mishap in Week Two of his rookie season, then got himself into a motorcycle accident that sidelined him for all of the following year. He did manage to put together a couple nice seasons but always seemed to represent a shadow of what had been possible—all while Ben Roethlisberger, whom the Browns whistled past to take Winslow, was leading the Steelers to playoff berth after playoff berth.

Similar scenario with wide receiver Braylon Edwards, who, aside from an incredible 2007 season, developed an unshakable reputation as a pass dropper extraordinaire over a tumultuous five-year career in Cleveland. All made possible because the Browns decided Aaron Rodgers, drafted by Green Bay shortly after Edwards in 2005, wasn't their quarterback of the future. The trend would continue into the next decade, underscored by the Browns trading away the sixth overall pick in 2011 to the Atlanta Falcons, opting not to pick dazzling wide receiver Julio Jones. The Falcons took Jones instead, and he quickly became one of the most explosive and exciting playmakers in the league. The Browns went with defensive tackle Phil Taylor, who made little impact after his first season and was released three years later. While they were at it, they decided eventual superstar defensive end J.J. Watt wasn't worth their while, either.

For a franchise that is perpetually (almost obsessively) drafting quarterbacks, they can't land a good one, even in a buyer's market. In back-to-back seasons, they passed up the chance to take first Carson Wentz in 2016, then Deshaun Watson in 2017—both of whom became instant stars with Philadelphia and Houston, respectively.

Even when the Browns tried to leverage the draft to acquire proven veterans, things tend to go horribly wrong. Take the bizarre saga of Davone Bess, who'd established himself as a dependable wide receiver in five years with Miami. During the 2013 draft, the Browns traded a pair of draft picks for Bess, who then delivered the worst season of his career, highlighted less by what he did on the field than what he did off it. After missing the final two games of the year to deal with a "personal matter," he posted a photo of himself on Twitter posing with what appeared to be a bag of marijuana. Shortly after, he was arrested for assaulting a police officer in an airport, and twelve hours after that, he took to Twitter once again, this time to share a picture of himself naked. His family then revealed that he'd been hospitalized against his will for similarly strange behavior six weeks before he was traded to Cleveland. Amazingly, it appeared the Browns were unaware of Bess's psychological struggles when they made the trade, reflected by a three-year, $11 million contract extension they extended to a player they then released less than a year later.

Even when the Browns apparently got lucky in the draft, it quickly turned into a flaming oil well. They rolled the dice on troubled wide receiver Josh Gordon, who'd shown amazing potential at Baylor but could never stay out of trouble, primarily because of an inability to resist the siren song of cannabis (plus popping Xanax, using counterfeit money, stealing credit cards, drug trafficking, and grand theft auto). The Browns grabbed him in the 2012 supplemental draft, and he put together an impressive rookie season. Six months later, he racked up the first of what would become a caboodle of violations of the NFL's drug policy, earning a two-game suspension to start the 2013 season. Even with the late start, Gordon exploded into stardom, leading the league with 1,646 receiving yards. He was named first team All-Pro, and it looked like the Browns had finally shown some draft cunning and caught a break. Neither turned out to be true.

The good feeling was gone before training camp opened the following year. In July, Gordon was arrested for DWI, then picked up his second substance-abuse violation and was suspended for the entire season, though it was eventually dropped to just ten games. After a one-game suspension for violating team rules to close out the year, a month later he tested positive for alcohol use, scoring a second straight year-long suspension. After sitting out 2015, his application for reinstatement was denied because—surprise, surprise—he failed another drug test. He entered rehab rather than trying to come back in 2016, but his reinstatement was turned down once again the following spring.

Six months later, the league, either overly forgiving or extremely forgetful, decided the sixth time would be the charm and reinstated Gordon on a conditional basis for the final six games of the 2017 season. Whether due to three years of seeing no game action or a reflection of the pitiful state of the Browns upon his return, Gordon showed little of the previously seen potential, catching only eighteen passes for an average of just over fifty yards per game. The good news was that he'd managed to stay clean for several months (exactly how long depended on which interview you read). On the other hand, he and his agent now seemed primarily interested in profiting on his sketchy past by selling his story of perpetual bad choices and incinerated opportunities instead of trying to salvage what should have been an amazing football career.

While the long, exasperating narrative of Josh Gordon was different from that of the Browns' other draft failures, the end result was the same: for most of his career, he was simply another extremely talented player *not* playing for the Cleveland Browns.

Teams pass up talented players destined for greatness every year. But perhaps no team has left more talent on the board than the Cleveland Browns. You can essentially set your watch by it: every draft, the Browns will pass over someone who will become a star in order to draft someone who won't come anywhere close. Sometimes it's because of bad luck, sometimes because of their own ineptitude. The Browns have somehow managed to become both the schlemiel and the schlimazel. And the cunning ability of Paul Brown to gauge talent and build a team from the ground up is as long gone as ancient Mesopotamia.

But while the Browns suffered, stumbled, and staggered in the draft, the Bengals used it to turn their franchise into a rogues' gallery.

***

One of the oft-repeated stories of Paul Brown's legacy centers around the Browns' first genuine off-field scandal in 1946.

A week before the Browns' first appearance in the All-America

Conference title game, a trio of players were involved in an argument with Cleveland police officers. The players were arrested and charged with creating a disturbance and public intoxication, and news of the incident broke the following day. At the next team meeting, Paul Brown kicked Jim Daniell, a starter and team captain who may have instigated the incident, off the team, and Daniell would never play professional football again. Many thought Brown was overreacting. But he felt it was warranted—because Daniell was a captain, Brown explained, he had an added responsibility to be a role model for the rest of the players. While, in retrospect, some argued that Brown was more willing to let Daniell go because he had an equally talented backup who could fill in without the Browns missing a beat, the overarching message was clear: there would be no tolerance for embarrassing incidents or encounters with law enforcement.

Over the next fifty years, things certainly changed in professional football. By 2000, even if a star player were charged with murder (here's looking at you, Ray Lewis), a team would hang onto him. And make him the face of the franchise. And erect a statue of him outside the stadium when his career was over.

One can only imagine what Paul Brown would have thought of this. Or what his reaction would be to the group mugshot his Bengals would become.

The trend began even before the new millennium. In 1992, a woman named Victoria Crytzer sued twenty Bengals for sexual assault at a Seattle hotel, claiming each player named either raped her or stood by while it happened. Her credibility soon came under attack, and her suit was dismissed—not based on a lack of evidence, but rather because she'd already accepted a settlement from the accused players in exchange for not pursuing legal action. Yet through it all, Crytzer would maintain her accusation was true. Following the decision, Bengals running back Ickey Woods, one of the accused, did his trademark posttouchdown "Shuffle" outside the courthouse—demonstrating a general insensitivity to the severity of the situation and forecasting the Bengals' long-standing inability to correctly read the room.

Then, mammoth defensive tackle Dan "Big Daddy" Wilkinson, the No. 1 overall draft pick out of Ohio State in 1994, was arrested for punching his pregnant girlfriend in the stomach the following year. He pled no contest and avoided jail time, as well as any type of team or league suspension. Which wasn't unusual for the NFL at the time. Mike Brown—offering the type of mob-lawyer sound bite he'd master over the years to come—pooh-poohed the whole thing, calling the incident "a blemish."

For the Bengals, it was a starting gun. Reflecting an overarching problem that would cast a shadow over the entire NFL, from 2000 on, Bengals players would be arrested eight times on charges of domestic violence. (Worse, there were rumors that the team advised the victimized wives and girlfriends to call team officials rather than police following an incident. If true, there's no way of knowing how many additional domestic violence episodes took place and were neatly swept under the Bengal-striped carpet.)

The franchise nurtured its devil-may-care reputation a few years later with another first-round draft pick: wide receiver Peter Warrick from Florida State, who carried with him the baggage from a much-publicized arrest for shoplifting and subsequent two-game suspension during his senior season. But compared to what was to come, this was like a Happy Meal version of a scandal. That same year, Bengals linebacker Steve Foley was arrested twice in two months, and star running back Corey Dillon was taken in for punching his wife in the mouth.

Over the next decade and a half, the Bengals' legal incidents ran the gamut. Theft, obstruction, probation violation, drunken driving, drunken boating, guns, marijuana, public urination, resisting arrest, disorderly conduct, and the disturbingly diverse category of "assault." You know there's a problem when your *kicker* is arrested for choking a guy in a bar. The low point was an eight-day stretch in July 2011, when three different Bengals were arrested in three separate incidents. In fact, between 2000 and 2013, the Bengals were tied for the league lead with forty player arrests, and the number would swell to forty-four by 2017.

The Bengals hit triple cherries on the criminal justice slot machine when they drafted wide receiver Chris Henry in 2005. Over the next three years, he would be arrested six times, with charges involving drugs, a gun, a DUI, and assault. Tragically (though not all that surprisingly), he died in the middle of a domestic dispute in December 2009 when he fell out of a moving pickup truck driven by his fiancée.

As if seeking to fill the void as the team's official legal lightning rod, five months later, the Bengals signed cornerback Adam "Pacman" Jones, who was basically a human Chernobyl. Since he'd joined the league five years before, he'd been involved in no fewer than ten incidents, at one point receiving a year-long suspension from the NFL. He kept up the pace with the Bengals with four more run-ins with the law, topped by a bizarre incident at a Cincinnati hotel in January 2017 in which he poked a security guard in the eye, then invited the arresting officer to get better acquainted with Jones's masculine anatomy. Presumably after the officer declined the offer, Jones then opined that he hoped the officer died the next day. TMZ Sports obtained and released a video showing the arrest that allowed the world to see just how ugly the incident really was.

But Mike Brown, ever patient with his hodgepodge of non-law-abiding players, stood behind Jones, offering him a second . . . or fifteenth . . . chance. "He regrets it," Brown explained afterward. "But it's been made into a public issue, and maybe I am overly tolerant. If so, so be it."

So be it? Mike Brown's laissez-faire attitude in this entire arena over the previous twenty-five years had turned his father's team into the Legion of Doom, to the point that the stripes on their helmets had come to represent something else entirely.

Three months after Jones's hotel meltdown, the Bengals once again demonstrated their abject tone deafness. In the second round of the draft, they selected Oklahoma running back Joe Mixon, whose claim to fame was less his football ability than his being caught on video punching a woman in the face three years earlier—celebrating his eighteenth birthday by inflicting a broken jaw. After being suspended for his freshman season, he followed it up with another incident involving a parking lot attendant who'd written him a ticket. He responded by ripping it up, throwing it in her face, and inching his car up to her to intimidate her.

The Bengals leadership—by now quite familiar with this particular brand of douchebaggery—was impressed with the way Mixon handled, as Marvin Lewis put it, "one day in a man's life" and determined, as with Jones, Henry, and a few dozen others, that it wouldn't happen again.

Even if that turns out to be true, you've got to wonder why a franchise that had spent the better part of the previous two decades combating a reputation as a thug factory would make such a mind-boggling move. Particularly since their track record in "rehabilitating" such problem cases was, shall we say, not outstanding.

Despite the cornucopia of PR black eyes the team suffered over the years, you could argue that the players' problems off the field had no real impact on what happened on the field.

That is, until January 2016, when the Bengals' on- and off-field worlds collided in one of the ugliest nights in NFL history.

***

Through the handful of successful, title-caliber seasons the Bengals had enjoyed in their history, they'd never been as dominant as they were in the fall of 2015. They won their first eight games—their best start ever—and stood at 10–2 entering the final month of the schedule. And, as always seems to be the case whenever the Bengals have something cooking, the Pittsburgh Steelers came along and wrecked it.

After Andy Dalton threw an interception on Cincinnati's first possession in a Week Fourteen showdown with the Steelers, he broke his thumb on the ensuing tackle. After eighty-one straight starts over his five-year career, Dalton's best season was abruptly over. The Bengals turned to untested backup AJ McCarron, who looked good in the final few games, and they hung on to capture the AFC North crown, matching a franchise-best twelve victories. Even without Dalton, there was a general agreement that this was the best Bengals team in the Marvin Lewis era, the franchise's optimal shot to get to the Super Bowl.

Waiting for them in the first round of the playoffs were—naturally— the Pittsburgh Steelers. Despite the black-and-yellow mojo the Steelers had held over the Bengals for the better part of the previous forty-plus years, it appeared as though Cincinnati's long playoff drought would finally come to an end on a rainy Saturday night in January. Rallying from a 15–0 fourth-quarter deficit, Cincinnati took the lead on an A.J. Green touchdown reception with 1:50 remaining, and the Paul Brown

Stadium faithful roared, tasting the team's first playoff victory in twenty-five years.

The deal was all but sealed on the next play from scrimmage, when Cincinnati linebacker Vontaze Burfict—one in the long line of Bengals players with a troubling history of behavior problems, including multiple suspensions and thousands of dollars in fines for dirty play—intercepted a pass at the Pittsburgh 26 with just 1:36 left to play. It seemed the Bengals' demons had been exorcised, and the game was in the bag.

But then, whatever has haunted the team since August 5, 1991, intervened once again.

On first down, with his only job simply to hold onto the football, Cincinnati running back Jeremy Hill fumbled, and the Steelers recovered. Ben Roethlisberger, who'd left the game with an injured shoulder, returned to the field to attempt to heroically lead the Steelers to victory. Not able to throw the ball long or even particularly well due to the injury, Roethlisberger dinked-and-dunked his way to the Cincinnati 47 with twenty-two seconds left. Out of time-outs, Roethlisberger fired another pass that was incomplete, but Burfict—who just moments before was set to be a hero—reverted back into *Hunger Games*-mode. As the football sailed uncatchable over the outstretched arms of Pittsburgh receiver Antonio Brown, Burfict lowered his helmet and charged straight into Brown's head, snapping it backward. In that moment, most remembered that Burfict had ended Steelers star running back Le'Veon Bell's season two months earlier with a hit that blew out a knee—then appeared to celebrate Bell's injury after the play. This time, Burfict was flagged for a fifteen-yard unnecessary roughness penalty for the blow on Brown, which caused a concussion, and Burfict would eventually be suspended three games.

Then, beyond belief, things got worse. In the aftermath of the play, Pittsburgh linebackers coach Joey Porter came onto the field to check on Brown and wound up getting into an argument with the poster child of the Bengals' behavior problems, Pacman Jones. Jones, who'd already gone berserk over the call and lashed out wildly at the officials, was penalized fifteen more yards for unsportsmanlike conduct. Down to their last breath, the Steelers wound up advancing thirty yards without running a play.

It was all they needed. On the next play, Pittsburgh kicked the winning field goal, and just like that, the Bengals had lost their eighth straight playoff game—marking the fifth straight season with a one-and-done ouster. "Resurrecting reasons to believe gets harder every year," Paul Daugherty wrote in the *Enquirer*. "The Bengals aren't the Cubs. We don't find their losing lovable."

It was undoubtedly the ugliest loss in franchise history. There were calls by fans and the media for Marvin Lewis—who, remember, had just led the Bengals to the best record in their history—to be fired. On a grand stage, he had lost whatever lax control he'd had over the emotional time bombs he'd collected over the years. And after more than twenty years of whistling past the graveyard of their players' character flaws, the Bengals' chickens had finally come home to roost.

To lose a playoff game in such a fashion was a clear indication of a raging cancer growing within the franchise. But, of course, Mike Brown initiated no drastic changes. The following season, Lewis was still on the sideline, and the erratic and morally challenged Bengals in question were still on the roster—Jones to be arrested yet again, Burfict to land a five-game suspension for another dirty hit a year later. Perhaps still haunted by the events of their playoff meltdown, the Bengals slipped to six victories in 2016 and then managed just seven in 2017, missing the playoffs in back-to-back seasons for the first time in a decade. With the window of opportunity for a title now apparently closed and attendance dipping drastically, it appeared that the Marvin Lewis era would finally come to an end. Many media outlets even broke the news late in the season that Lewis would not return as head coach. But two days after the season ended, he signed a two-year contract with the Bengals, stunning (and angering) many fans who were desperate for change.

Yet the Bengals' sudden collapse and puzzling decision to stay the course was not the most embarrassing pro football story in Ohio. That dubious distinction belonged to the Cleveland Browns, who'd managed to follow up a horrendous 3–13 season in 2015 with even worse. After hiring Bengals offensive coordinator Hue Jackson (there he is again, gang) as their new head coach—Jimmy Haslam's fourth in five seasons—the Browns were cautiously optimistic they'd take a step forward in 2016—particularly in the midst of a magical sports year in Cleveland that saw the Cavaliers win the city's first world title in fifty-two years and a plucky Indians team defy the odds to reach the seventh game of the World Series.

The Browns, meanwhile, managed to reach the seventh circle of hell. They lost their first fourteen games, and watching them play became like an unanesthetized dental procedure. By November, the only genuine topic of conversation centered around whether or not they'd become just the second NFL team to post an 0–16 record. Darkly sardonic plans for a "Perfect Season" parade if the Browns went winless began taking shape.

But, as usual, the Browns went and spoiled everybody's fun by winning a Christmas Eve cacophony with San Diego, simply because the equally bumbling Chargers failed to convert a pair of potentially game-tying field goals in the final four minutes. The parade, and the comic, tongue-in-cheek catharsis that might have resulted from it, was cancelled, and the Browns finished 1–15—somehow managing to find the only thing worse than finishing winless.

But even after failing at abject failure, the Browns got right back on their inept horse and tried again in 2017. The losses continued to spread like shingles, and the only thing that genuinely distinguished this year from the previous one was a massive debacle at the trading deadline that seemed to take place with circus music playing in the background. An agreed transaction with Cincinnati to acquire Bengals backup quarterback AJ McCarron fell apart because the Browns failed to send their approval of the trade before the deadline. Better still, the reason they missed the deadline was either because of a rudimentary mix-up in sending the confirmation email, or that, reportedly, Browns executives were too busy celebrating the trade to complete it. Either way, it was yet another display of crippling incompetence that by now was simply par for the course.

This time around, there was no holiday intervention to save them from historic infamy. Once again inexplicably finding a new low beneath a steaming pile of apocalypse, they closed out a perfectly imperfect season and became the NFL's second 0–16 team. It completed a mind-boggling string of thirty-four losses in thirty-five games and the worst three-year stretch for any pro football team in more than seventy years with a deplorable 4–44 record. The parade Cleveland didn't deserve but sort of needed finally happened, ironically celebrating their once-beloved, once-respected football team anchoring its reputation as the most mortifying franchise in professional sports.

Some would argue that now, finally at the ultimate rock bottom, at least there's no way things could get worse. To which the Browns will likely respond, "Hold my beer." After willy-nilly firings of coaches who'd provided better results and seemed to offer some hope for improvement, Jimmy Haslam announced that a 1–31 record was good enough for him to bring Hue Jackson back for a third season—which, perhaps appropriately, reflects the longest tenure of any Browns coach under Haslam's ownership. In the upside-down world of Truck Stop Jimmy Haslam, it all makes perfect sense.

As did using the No. 1 overall pick of the draft three months later to select controversial Oklahoma University quarterback Baker Mayfield—best known for an on-field crotch-grab taunt and an off-field public intoxication arrest. Not only did he appear to be a warped *Westworld* doppleganger of Johnny Manziel, but he represented various aspects of every draft mistake the Browns had ever made—in essence, the Voltron of all their failed first-round quarterbacks. Time will tell if he'll turn out to be yet another disaster (or, more likely, what flavor of disaster he'll wind up becoming).

Ultimately, the real tragedy in Cleveland isn't the embarrassing play or the lack of continuity or the Choose Your Own Adventure front-office decisions, but rather that the Browns of the last two-plus decades have completely redefined the franchise's reputation and legacy. The Browns are now just a few years away from dragging their all-time win-loss record—which, remember, stood at .627 after nearly a half century of play prior to Paul Brown's death—beneath the .500 mark for the first time ever. Now, when people think of the Browns, they don't think of success, but rather of colossal failure. They don't think of the Browns notching nineteen winning records in their first twenty NFL seasons, but rather staggering to eighteen losing records in their last twenty. They're much more likely to think of Johnny Manziel or Peyton Hillis before they think of Otto Graham or Jim Brown. And they realize that

Randy Lerner and Jimmy Haslam have now left nearly as big an imprint on the franchise as Paul Brown.

Cleveland and the Browns have become a real-life *Pet Sematary* allegory. In the classic Stephen King story, the main character attempts to cheat death by burying the deceased in a cursed Indian burial ground. The dead then return, looking just as they had before, but now as stinking, soulless nightmares with the sole purpose of killing everything around them.

These are the new Cleveland Browns.

The harsh truth is that the franchise that Paul Brown molded into a civic touchstone tragically died four years after its namesake when the franchise was uprooted and moved to Baltimore. But rather than mourning the death and moving on, in desperation, the city and fans interred the corpse in the cursed burial ground of expansion, hoping for a second chance. And indeed, the franchise did return, looking much like the Browns of old, but it became very apparent very quickly that these Browns were just a rotted, defiled version of their former selves. And after nearly two decades of unrealistically consistent and unprecedented failure, it seems they always will be.

The tortured fans of Cleveland are reminded of this every single Sunday, every single season, and ruefully wonder if bringing the Browns back was the right decision.

"Sometimes," as a character explains in King's novel, "dead is better."

$$***$$

In Shakespearean terms, Paul Brown's passing in 1991 was the death of Mercutio in *Romeo and Juliet*. Just as Mercutio's dying words cursed both the rival Montagues and Capulets, it's as if Paul Brown's cast a plague on both the Browns' and Bengals' houses. And they haven't been the same since.

"The whole state shared the glow of Paul Brown's fame during football season," columnist Bill Livingston wrote in the *Plain Dealer* the day Brown died. "In Cleveland, especially, the sense that Terminal Tower really had fallen was palpable ... Perhaps Paul Brown's passing hurt here more than in any other place in Ohio, because we know more than any-one else how impossible he is to replace."

Obviously, Paul Brown *was* replaced within the Bengals organiza-tion, just as he'd been replaced in the Cleveland organization twenty-eight years earlier. But to say that things changed would be a laughable understatement.

In a metaphysical sense, it's as if he never really went away. In the years since his passing, Paul Brown has hovered as a specter over both of the franchises he created. Not necessarily with malicious or vindictive intent, but rather as an embodiment of disapproval and disappointment.

The bald-headed master from Massillon was hard and occasion-ally harsh, but not, by character, vengeful. So to accuse the old coach of "cursing" his former teams might be off the mark. "Paul Brown would never raise his voice," Otto Graham said the day Brown died. "He'd just stare at you with those cold, steely eyes that went right through you. And that was worse."

In essence, this is what Paul Brown has been doing to the Browns and Bengals ever since he died, and it's those cold eyes staring at them from beyond the grave that continue to haunt both teams. It's a figura-tive haunting in that he left an incredible legacy that would be nearly impossible for them to match. And a literal haunting in that . . . well, perhaps he's using supernatural means to prevent them from achieving undeserved success.

So how can this be resolved?

For years, many Cincinnati fans have contended it's a simple matter of Mike Brown selling the team. Browns fans see it as more than that, perhaps calling for the need to delve into the occult a smidge more by, say, offering some sort of sacrifice at Paul Brown's grave.

Maybe erecting a statue is the trick, like the ones that honor him at his alma maters of Massillon and Miami University. But that raises the question of where to put it—Cleveland or Cincinnati? When asked point-blank in 2013, Marvin Lewis responded frankly: "[Answering] politically, there would be two, right?" His nonpolitical answer fol-lowed—since the Bengals already honored him by naming their sta-dium after him, the statue should go in Cleveland (perhaps spiritually atoning for callously taking his name off their stadium). And indeed, a

Plain Dealer poll two years later revealed that 47 percent of respondents felt Brown deserved a statue over any other figure in team history—doubling the response for running back Jim Brown, who then received a statue in 2016. The missed opportunities continue to pile up.

Perhaps there should be a Paul Brown museum, stemming off the temporary exhibition at the Massillon Museum in 2016. Or maybe it's a matter of paranormal extermination rather than education—some sort of football exorcism, maybe with Max Von Sydow donning a chinstrap instead of a cassock.

Maybe it's bigger than just the Browns and Bengals. Maybe Paul Brown is upset that modern fans have more respect for a handful of inferior, made-for-TV coaches than himself or the other giants who built the game. Thus, he lashes out angrily and ectoplasmically at his former teams as a way of drawing attention to his tragically fading legacy. Or perhaps he punishes the Browns and Bengals as a way of reminding us that he brought these teams into the world, and dammit, he can take them out.

What's truly heartbreaking about this multigenerational double-downturn is that Ohio utterly loves football. When you factor in its passion at every level of the game, Ohio is genuinely cuckoo for gridiron Cocoa Puffs as much or more so than any other state in the Union. And Paul Brown is unquestionably its football George Washington.

Each team has supplied a revolving door of different coaches, different players, different stadiums, and, in the Browns' case at least, different owners. Yet their combined lot remains the same.

Whatever the answer, it feels as though the Browns and Bengals must join forces to find it. To see if there's a way to put aside their disdain for each other and come together to find a solution that will be mutually beneficial to both.

Perhaps the biblical allusions deep within the Browns-Bengals rivalry can point the way. For all the hatred and agony that was born out of the followers of Isaac and Ishmael, the two rival sons finally did come together.

To bury their father.

SOURCES

Books

Brown, Paul with Clary, Jack, *PB: The Paul Brown Story*, New York: Atheneum, 1979.

Cantor, George, *Paul Brown: The Man Who Invented Modern Football*, Chicago: Triumph Books, 2008.

Collett, Ritter, *Super Stripes: PB and the Super Bowl Bengals*, Dayton, OH: Landfall Press, 1982.

Gregg, Forrest and O'Toole, Andrew, *Winning in the Trenches*, Cincinnati, OH: Clerisy Press, 2009.

Harris, David, *The Genius: How Bill Walsh Reinvented Football and Created an NFL Dynasty*, New York: Random House, 2008.

Heaton, Chuck, *Browns Scrapbook: A Fond Look Back at Five Decades of Football, from a Legendary Cleveland Sportswriter*, Cleveland, OH: Gray & Company, 2007.

Knight, Jonathan, *Kardiac Kids: The Story of the 1980 Cleveland Browns*, Kent, OH: Kent State University Press, 2003.

Knight, Jonathan, *Sundays in the Pound: The Heroics and Heartbreak of the 1985-1989 Cleveland Browns*, Kent, OH: Kent State University Press, 2006.

Knight, Jonathan, *The Browns Bible: The Complete Game-by-Game History of the Cleveland Browns*, Kent, OH: Kent State University Press, 2013.

Levy, Bill, *Sam, Sipe, & Company: The Story of the Cleveland Browns*, Cleveland, OH: J.T. Zubal & P.D. Dole, Publishers,1981.

MacCambridge, Michael, *America's Game: The Epic Story of How Pro Football Captured a Nation*, New York: Random House, 2004.

Morgan, Jon, *Glory for Sale: Fans, Dollars and the New NFL*, Baltimore, MD: Bancroft Press, 1997.

O'Toole, Andrew, *Paul Brown: The Rise and Fall and Rise Again of Football's Most Innovative Coach*, Cincinnati, OH: Clerisy Press, 2008.

Piascik, Andy, *The Best Show in Football: The 1946-1955 Cleveland Browns*, New York: Taylor Trade Publishing, 2007.

Pluto, Terry, *False Start: How the New Browns Were Set Up to Fail*, Cleveland, OH: Gray & Company, 2004.

Poplar, Michael G. with Toman, James A., *Fumble! The Browns, Modell and the Move: An Insider's Story*, Cleveland, OH: Landmarks Press, 1997.

Rutigliano, Sam, *Pressure*, Nashville, TN: Oliver Nelson Books, 1988.

Snyder, John and Conner, Floyd, *Day By Day in Cincinnati Bengals History*, New York: Leisure Press, 1984.

Walsh, Bill with Jamison, Steve and Walsh, Craig, *The Score Takes Care of Itself*, New York: Portfolio, 2009.

Magazines

Browns News/Illustrated
Cincinnati City Beat
Cincinnati Magazine
Cleveland Scene
Crain's Cleveland Business
Forbes
Rolling Stone

Sports Illustrated
The Sporting News

Newspapers

Cleveland Plain Dealer
Cleveland Press
Cincinnati Enquirer
Cincinnati Post
Denver Post
Los Angeles Times
New York Daily News
New York Times
Seattle Times
Tampa Bay Times
The Times-Picayune
USA Today
Wall Street Journal
Washington Post

Internet Sources

10News, 10news.com
Arrest Nation, arrestnation.com
Bengals Jungle, bengalsjungle.com
BengalsZone, forums.bengalszone.com
Bleacher Report, bleacherreport.com
Business Insider, businessinsider.com
CBS Sports, cbssports.com
Cincinnati Bengals, bengals.com
Cincy Jungle, cincyjungle.com
Cleveland Frowns, clevelandfrowns.com
Deadspin, deadspin.com
ESPN, espn.com
Football Zebras, footballzebras.com
FOX Sports, foxsports.com

God Awful NFL Teams, godawfulnflteams.com
Mike Brown Sucks, mikebrownsucks.com
National Football League, NFL.com
Orange and Brown Report, scout.com/nfl/browns
Pro Football Reference, pro-football-reference.com
SB Nation, sbnation.com
WCPO, wcpo.com
Your Team Cheats, yourteamcheats.com
YouTube, youtube.com

Wire Services

Associated Press

Other

Cincinnati Bengals media guides
Cleveland Browns media guides